**DO NOT REMOVE
CARDS FROM POCKET**

The Future of Housing Markets

A NEW APPRAISAL

ENVIRONMENT, DEVELOPMENT, AND PUBLIC POLICY

A series of volumes under the general editorship of
Lawrence Susskind, *Massachusetts Institute of Technology*
Cambridge, Massachusetts

CITIES AND DEVELOPMENT

Series Editor: Lloyd Rodwin, *Massachusetts Institute of Technology*
Cambridge, Massachusetts

Other subseries:

ENVIRONMENTAL POLICY AND PLANNING

Series Editor: Lawrence Susskind, *Massachusetts Institute of Technology*
Cambridge, Massachusetts

PUBLIC POLICY AND SOCIAL SERVICES

Series Editor: Gary Marx, *Massachusetts Institute of Technology*
Cambridge, Massachusetts

The Future of Housing Markets

A NEW APPRAISAL

Leland S. Burns
and
Leo Grebler

University of California, Los Angeles
Los Angeles, California

PLENUM PRESS • NEW YORK AND LONDON

Library of Congress Cataloging in Publication Data

Burns, Leland Smith.
  The future of housing markets.

  (Environment, development, and public policy. Cities and development)
  Bibliography: p.
  Includes index.
    1. Housing policy—United States. 2. Housing—United States—Forecasting. I.
  Grebler, Leo. II. Title. III. Series.
  HD7293.B88   1986   339.4′869083′0973   86-20541
  ISBN 0-306-42313-8

© 1986 Plenum Press, New York
A Division of Plenum Publishing Corporation
233 Spring Street, New York, N.Y. 10013

Printed in the United States of America

Preface

This book's title betrays at once that it belongs in the forecast literature. Peering into the future is a notoriously treacherous venture. Nevertheless, it has become a practice endemic to the business and government worlds as well as to academia, especially economics. We like to believe that the enormous growth of forecasting in the face of some disappointments reflects real needs of decision-makers (as well as the general public's well-warranted curiosity about the future). Fashion alone could hardly explain the sustained increase in the market for forecast services during the past few decades.

Some professionals insist on fine distinctions between the forecast, the projection, the prediction—and the prophecy. The differences are more semantic than real, as the mandatory resort to Webster confirms. The entry "forecast" includes references to prediction and prophecy without differentiation, while "projection" is defined, among other things, as prediction or "advance estimate." We use mainly the term *projections* because much of our statistical research is based on forward estimates of population and households by the U.S. Bureau of the Census which the bureau itself, the greatest fountain of data in the world, records as projections.

This study, however, is intended to show not only *what* will happen in the housing market but also *why* it will happen. Hence, we must deal with a range of social phenomena that influence the market: the varying ways in which people group themselves in households, preferences for togetherness and solo living, the durability of marriage, and the growing number of women who work outside the home, to name a few. The portions of the book that try to project social change rely partly on judgments—we hope, informed judgments—so we do not object to the label "prophecy" despite the slightly malodorous connotation of the word in scholarly literature.

While the semantic classification of this study is of tangential interest, the ingredients for any responsible forecast, prediction, projection, prophecy are not. One essential ingredient is a thorough understanding of the past. This is true no less for trend projections like those offered here than for the short-term forecasts in business-cycle research. The dire consequences of ignoring history have been so often cited, notably in the words of the philosopher George Santayana, that they need not be restated. In the case at hand, this means reliance on the analysis and synthesis of large quantities of information about housing markets and their socioeconomic determinants since World War II. We have made an effort to ease the reader's burden by presenting the statistical evidence in ways that allow the analytical points to surface quickly. But our extensive array of historical facts and figures is not dictated by a belief that they can be simply extrapolated into future trends. On the contrary, this study was initiated in the expectation of a marked change in the long-run demographic conditions on which housing depends, and its results show an admixture of continuous and discontinuous socioeconomic forces bearing on future housing markets.

Another essential requirement of responsible forecasting is to set boundaries for the scope of what is being projected. This volume focuses on those changes in prospective housing demand that are shaped by demographic and emergent social forces. In contrast to other studies of the same type, it does not proceed to estimate the future volume of residential construction. In our view, such an estimate is not only hazardous but of highly questionable utility. In addition to household formation, already influenced by economic conditions and social changes, any projection of new housing units must take account of two factors extremely difficult to predict for 10-year or longer periods: replacement demand and net conversions.

Replacement demand, usually figured to equal the net loss of dwelling units from the stock, varies enormously over time. Net losses in the 1960s came to 6.9 million housing units. In the 1970s they were only 2.6 million, or 38% of the volume reported for the previous decade. For the 1980s, respected analysts have come up with projections ranging between 7 million and 12 million. The amount of net conversions which add to the housing supply without new construction is wholly a matter of guesswork. Private forecasts for the 1980s vary between 1.2 and 3.5 million units.

Because of the extreme uncertainties of replacement and conversions as well as the future economic outlook, some conscientious forecasters have developed a range of projections for residential building activity. The range is apt to be so large that the usefulness of the results is seriously impaired. Besides, it is influenced by prospective policy decisions on housing subsidies. This study, however, is oriented to housing *markets* and not to social housing needs.

Our emphasis on the past and future demographic base for housing demand does not mean neglect of other factors. Prominent among these are an anticipated demand shift to higher-quality housing and the technological change that is beginning to transfer economic activities from the workplace to the residence, augmenting the functions performed by dwellings. Also, the contributions of household formation and of real per household income to consumer purchasing power, the source of housing investment, have varied greatly in the past. In the 1970s, household increases accounted for all of the rise in purchasing power, a quite unusual ratio. Changes in real per household income had a slightly negative effect. Under the projections, the picture will be vastly different in the future. Because of its anticipated decline, household formation will make a smaller contribution to consumer purchasing power, and a viable housing market will depend more heavily on real income growth, as it did before the decade of the 1970s. Hence, the general economic scenario will once again become a more crucial determinant of the demand for housing.

To many who helped in completing the research and producing the final version of the book, we are grateful. Scott Edmondson, David Etezadi, Scott Kutnar, and Marilou Uy provided research assistance funded by grants from the Committee on Research of the UCLA

Academic Senate. Frank Mittelbach helped by directing us to sources and stimulating and challenging our ideas. Rose Altman, Bernice Don, Nancy Kawata, and Etsu Otomo patiently and skillfully typed and retyped drafts. Shinji Isozaki prepared the charts. The Housing, Real Estate and Urban Land Studies Program at the UCLA Graduate School of Management generously made its facilities available for the study. As always, the authors alone bear the responsibility for the results.

Contents

List of Tables

CHAPTER 3

CHAPTER 4

CHAPTER 5

List of Figures

CHAPTER 1

CHAPTER 2

CHAPTER 3

CHAPTER 4

CHAPTER 5

1

Introduction

The housing market has recently staged a smart recovery from a severe and prolonged slump. Since cyclical swings are an ever-recurring feature of our economy, another housing recession may be around the corner as this is written. But the housing industry has come to be inured to the vicissitudes of cycles and can be expected to cope with the pains of a downturn, as it did so often in the past.

Meanwhile another adversity, quite different from a cyclical decline and certainly of longer duration, is appearing on the scene: The demographic support for long-run housing demand is eroding. This trend will continue through the rest of the 20th century and will affect the numerous business groups and public agencies associated with the development, improvement, and transfer of residential real estate:

- Builders of homes, apartments, and condominiums.

- Developers of sites for residential use.
- Contractors who perform alteration and modernization work.
- Investors in residential real estate.
- Construction and mortgage lenders.
- Real estate brokers, escrow companies, and others providing services for property transactions.
- Producers and distributors of building materials and of equipment items for old as well as new residential units.
- Architects, designers, and construction engineers.
- Planners, policy makers, and administrators of public programs.

Besides, if demographic forces induce a downward trend in the demand for housing, the repercussions will extend to the nation's economy as a whole and its financial markets. Because of the large multiplier effects of residential construction, nearly every major sector of the economy would feel the impact. Hence, a weakening of housing demand over a long period of time is a matter of universal concern.

Unfavorable demographic conditions for housing demand have for some time been anticipated by statisticians and researchers. Until recently, however, they were not expected to develop before the 1990s or, at the earliest, the last few years of the 1980s. During the current decade, it was widely believed, the vitality of the residential market would be sustained by the ''echo effects'' of the postwar baby boom, as it was during the 1970s. In contrast, projections by the U.S. Bureau of the Census indicate that adverse demographic changes are imminent.

We are entering a new era in which the echo effects of previous births on housing will differ markedly from those of the baby boom, reflecting the declining birth trend that began in the early 1960s. In 1980–1985, for example, the increase in the number of persons in the age group 18–34—the age of entry into the housing market—has been estimated at only 2.6 million as against 8.5 million during the preceding half decade. The sharp reduction in growth will be followed by actual decline through the year 2000 and possibly beyond. Young adults, of course, are of strategic importance to the establishment of households and the demand for separate dwelling units, regardless of whether individual members choose to marry or arrange themselves more informally in "twosomes" or stay single.

Thus, it has become a matter of considerable urgency to reassess the magnitude of projected population shifts affecting housing, analyze the market adjustments that are in store, and ponder ways and means of cushioning their impact on the housing industry. That is the purpose of the present study.

While demographic changes adverse to housing are already under way rather than postponed to the 1990s, our analysis will dispel fears of a great deterioration in housing demand. These fears reflect largely semantics. The decline in births after the postwar baby boom has been widely interpreted as a baby *bust.* Just as the delayed effects of the boom provided housing with a great tonic, those of a bust would have dire consequences. But the conventional assumption of an inevitable boom–bust sequence, derived from popular observation of business cycles, does not apply. Average annual births fell from 4 million in the 1946–1962 period to a little over 3.5 million in 1963–1983. A decline of about 12% hardly denotes a "bust." In contrast, the unusual increase of births during the postwar years does warrant the colloquial boom designation. Contrast the 15-year period running from the onset of the Great Depression to the end of World War II with the subsequent 15 years. The average number of births rose from 2.6 million between 1929 and 1945 to the 4 million recorded for 1946–1962, or by 54%.[1] The notable difference between the successive upward and downward movements of births is portrayed in Figure 1.1, which also shows the actual and projected number of persons 18–34 years old 25 years after the reported births, at about the age in life when the previous infants typically form their households. As one would expect, the two variables are highly correlated, although the group of young adults includes immigrants as well as the babies born in the United States who reach the first stage of adulthood.

With a moderate and gradual decrease of births between the early 1960s and early 1980s, the echo effects on housing can also be expected to be moderate and gradual rather than sudden and catastrophic. This is illustrated in Figure 1.1 by the gentle downward slope of the curve for the number of young adults between 1985 and 2000, our preliminary proxy for population changes affecting the demand for housing.

Some regions and subareas will face more severe adjustments than others, but such differences always exist in an economic sector composed of local markets. The housing industry in fast-growing regions will suffer little pain from the reversal of demographic trends; it will be in a less favorable position in slow-growing or stagnating areas. Hence, it is pertinent to note that the population shift to the so-called Sunbelt (the South and the

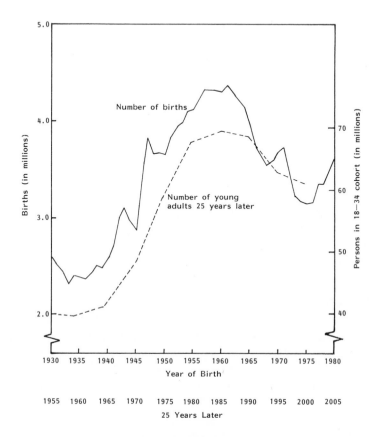

FIGURE 1.1. Annual number of births 1930–1980 and number of persons in 18–34 age cohort 25 years later, at half-decade benchmarks (source: U.S. Bureau of the Census, various years).

West), one of the widely discussed phenomena of recent decades, is expected to persist (Figure 1.2). According to preliminary estimates, the 1960 population of the South and West regions will double to 161 million at the turn of the century. In contrast, the Northeast and North

Central regions will just about hold their own. In the year 2000, the South and the West will account for 60% of the U.S. population compared to 46% 40 years earlier, with corresponding relative losses for the other regions. The shift is only in part explained by the movement of elderly people to the Sunbelt. At the turn of the century, the South and the West are also expected to account for 60% of all persons under 65 years of age.

Data problems and the constraints of space make it impossible to pursue differential area analysis of the consequences of the weakening demographic base for housing demand. The remainder of the study will necessarily be given over to national aggregates.

The next chapter traces the changing demographic conditions for housing demand in some detail. In additon to shifts in the age composition of the adult population that operate in disfavor of demand and slow the upward trend in total household formation, the chapter will highlight two key factors in the past growth of households. These are the marked increase in the number of families other than married couples—"truncated" families headed by a single man or woman rather than two spouses—and the even greater rise in the number of nonfamily households, usually composed of single persons living in separate dwelling units. The conjugal family, once considered the standard unit for housing demand and residential building, has lost its dominant position. Its share in total households, just short of 80% in 1950, dropped below 60% in 1984 and is expected to decline further. One of the crucial issues in projecting housing demand and especially in meeting the differentiated demands of various consumer units is the continuance of these trends and their future strength.

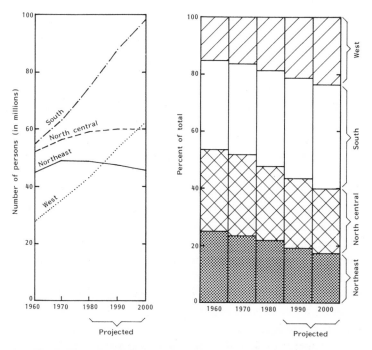

FIGURE 1.2. Growth and distribution of population by region, actual 1960–1980 and projected 1990–2000 (source: U.S. Bureau of the Census, 1985, Table 10, p. 10).

Chapter 3 deals with socioeconomic forces affecting household formation. During the past generation, most of these factors have favored the housing market, whatever their other impacts on society may have been. The increasing incidence of divorce, for example, has often produced a demand for two housing units instead of one. The rising number of women holding jobs outside the home has augmented family income and thereby stimulated the demand for better dwellings, or it has facilitated the establishment of separate households by single females. The accelerating numbers and proportions of people choosing to live alone has swelled the ranks of single-person households. Because the rate of household formation has by far exceeded the rate of population growth, the average size of housholds has been declining while the average size of housing units has remained about the same.

Can these and other trends with a positive influence on housing markets be projected into the future? Will they be as strongly supportive as they were in the past few decades? Or will they reverse their direction? Answers to such questions appear to be highly speculative, but two methods are used to strip them of many elements of guesswork. One is the observation of recent indicators of social change. The other is an analysis of the broad consequences of the shift from a large adult generation (the one produced by the postwar baby boom) to a smaller generation.

Underlying forces will shape the future of housing demand expressed not only in numbers of units built but in the ways that households use their dwellings. Changing household composition will reshape future preferences. Reduced household size and the extension of family life into many years without children in the home are bound to change demands for space. The radically altered proportion of women at home versus in the workplace will affect the kind and especially the design of dwellings consumers want. In general, we conclude that many of the socioeconomic trends that have stimulated housing demand during recent decades will persist but at a slower pace.

Chapter 4 presents a novel way of looking at residential demand by considering the typical housing decisions made by people at different stages of their life cycle. Since the change from favorable to unfavorable demographic conditions for housing market activity is caused by a notable shift in the age composition of the adult population, this type of analysis seems especially appropriate for studying future markets. One of the significant issues in assessing the magnitude of future demand, for example, is the question whether the prospective reduction in the number of young households can be offset by demand generated among older households that are already housed. To resolve or at least illuminate the question, one needs to examine the housing decisions faced by households as they pass through their life cycles, as well as the variables that bear at each stage on their housing decisions such as changes in household composition, labor force participation, income, and residential mobility (or the propensity to move at various ages). While economists are apt to use housing demand in the singular for most of their analytical work, emphasis on life-cycle stages serves to highlight the variety of housing *demands* as households progress from one age bracket to the next.

These demands differ, and they often differ substantially, among households at various stages of their life cycles. There are obvious distinctions not only between the types of housing suited to the requirements of young adults compared to seniors, but even between those in adjacent stages of the life cycle. Households in the 35–44 age group, for example, are concerned with increasing pressures put on their housing space, but their generally rising incomes allow them to choose between expanding the homes they occupy or purchasing larger houses. At the same time, those 10 years their junior are struggling to accumulate the capital required for even a reasonably modest down payment on a "starter" unit.

The ability of a household in any age group to exert effective demand for housing may change due to factors over which it has little or no control. The bettered economic circumstance of the elderly is a case in point. Fate, in the form of a benevolent public policy, has smiled on the elderly in recent years. The dramatic income increases enjoyed by seniors, largely as a consequence of rising Social Security payments, broadened pension coverage, and high interest rates on investment put today's oldsters in a far better position than their counterparts of even a decade ago.

Another quirk of fate affecting the translation of housing desires into effective demand is the luck of birth into a cohort that is blessed, or not, by special circumstances. One of these circumstances is simply the size of the age cohort. Just as it is better to be rich than it is to be poor, as Mae West claimed, it is better to belong to a small generation than to a large one, for being born during a period of low birth rates seems to convey advantages that continue to pay off throughout life. Much of the recent housing affordability crisis, plaguing young adults seeking entrance into the home ownership market, can be explained by the relatively large numbers of persons coming of age coupled with the poor earnings that result from an abundant supply of labor.

The final chapter develops the study's main thesis that rising demand for higher-quality dwellings will cushion the unfavorable demographic effects on future housing in the rest of this century. The yardstick for measuring the performance of the housing sector is shifted from the number of newly built units, the conventional standard, to residential investment. Because investment in constant dollars reflects quality changes through modernization of the existing stock—an activity that is projected to expand—as well as those incorporated in new construction, it represents a superior criterion for assessing the future of housing markets.

Quality improvements that raise the real input per housing unit are expected to come from the increase of middle-aged households with greater discretionary spending power; from the progressive use of equipment to mechanize household operations, stimulated by the upward trend of women in the paid labor force; and from the emerging transformation of the dwelling as a living place to a workplace. In the wake of technological innovations and the growth of professional services that do not require the common separation of residence and office or shop, the dwelling will perform new functions.

Modern technology will influence the future use of housing as it never did before because the economics of time, long recognized in organizing the production and distribution of goods and services, is becoming an important factor for consumers as well. As the value of work time rises with economic growth, consumers are motivated to economize on non-work time which, among other things, is absorbed by household management.

Similarly, the transfer of some work functions to the home will be dictated by time saving (as in the elimination of commuting) and will be facilitated by electronic workshops within the dwelling. Under the pressure of public demands, zoning ordinances that call for strict separation of residential and other land uses are likely to be revised (or else ignored). New functions of the dwelling and additional labor-saving devices within it will tend to increase the value of residences.

Under the influence of demographic forces and cost factors, notably the disproportionate rise of lot prices, homeownership is likely to stabilize at the current rate of two-thirds of all occupied housing units. The chapter proceeds to analyze future adjustments of housing suppliers to projected demand changes. None of the adjustments seem to necessitate drastic changes in the structure of suppliers, except that the producers of sophisticated household equipment will play a growing role and carry the main risks of technological advances.

The last chapter concludes with some comments on the general economic climate for housing through the year 2000. The comments focus on two problems that have pronounced effects on interest rates and are likely to persist in most of the projection period: the federal budget deficit and the specter of an international financial crisis resulting from the overindebtedness of some foreign countries to U.S. banks. Other maladjustments, such as the U.S. trade deficit and the uncertainties generated by the recent ad hoc policy of deregulating our financial system, are more amenable to early correction. If the special problems impeding economic growth potentials are solved or attenuated, the general scenario should at least provide a neutral base for housing progress, allowing the adverse demographic forces to work themselves out with minimum disturbance.

NOTES

1. Our selection of the periods of low, high, and declining births adopts the delineation by Masnick and Bane (1980, Table B.8). Given the data, there is no hard-and-fast rule for selecting benchmark years, but alternative groupings of the annual figures would not change the results significantly.

REFERENCES

Masnick, G. and Bane, M. J. (1980). *The nation's families: 1960–1990.* Boston: Auburn House.

U.S. Bureau of the Census. (various years). *Statistical abstract of the United States.* Washington, D.C.: U.S. Government Printing Office.

U.S. Bureau of the Census. (various years). *Vital statistics of the United States.* Washington, D.C.: U.S. Government Printing Office.

2

The Changing Demographic
Base of Housing Demand

This account of demographic forces affecting future housing demand is rendered in three parts. The first focuses on the projected decline in the number of young adults whose increase in the past two decades was a major factor in household formation. The second describes the slowing growth of households, the demand units for housing. The third portrays the continued shift in the composition of households in disfavor of the conjugal family, once the main source of rising demand for housing and especially for home ownership.

The link between housing and households is formed by definition: The Census Bureau counts as a household the group of persons (or the single individual) who occupy a separate housing unit. Thus, with the number of households at any given time equaling the number of occupied dwelling units, any assessment of long-run housing demand rests on household formation.

The projections of population and households presented here are those of the Bureau of the Census. While some analysts have been critical of certain assumptions and methods of the bureau and have developed alternative estimates,[1] recent revisions have made the official projections more acceptable. In any event, this study requires no more than general indicators of the direction and approximate magnitude of demographic changes bearing on future housing demand. The census data meet these requirements in entirely adequate fashion. The "middle series" of their several population projections is used throughout the analysis. The differences resulting from the adoption of the lowest and highest series, discussed in Appendix A, are quite small for the forecast period.

DECLINE OF THE YOUNG ADULT GENERATION

The spectacular increase of young adults (18 to 34 years) in the 1960s and 1970s, from 39 million to nearly 68 million, will reverse itself quite sharply and, as Figure 2.1 shows, the reversal has already begun. In 1980–1985 the age group 18–34 gains by only 2.6 million persons as against 8.5 million during the preceding 5-year period and 9.4 million 5 years before that. Looking ahead, the number of young adults will decrease after 1985. Although the 61 million estimated for the year 2000 still exceeds the 1975 level, the reversed growth trend of the young adult generation is critical to the future course of housing demand. In the 1970s, this group furnished the most active participants in the market, entering it as renters or home buyers, changing from rental to owner-

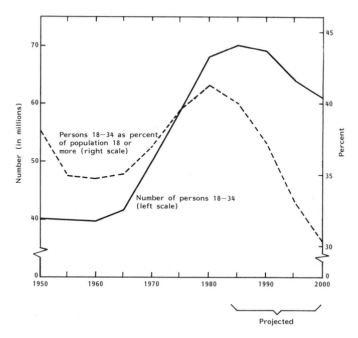

FIGURE 2.1. Young adults (18–34 years), number and percent of all adults, 5-year intervals, 1950–2000 (source: Table B.1).

ship status, and upgrading their housing accommodations as real incomes increased with job experience or advancement.

The proportion of young adults to all adults will decline drastically from a 1980 peak exceeding 40% to 30% in 2000. This is their lowest share in the total recorded at any time during the half century portrayed in the figure. The relative decline reflects not only the diminishing ranks of young adults that mirror the falling number of births during the 1960s and most of the 1970s but also the swelling ranks of older people as the generation born during the postwar baby boom matures.

The most obvious feature of the changes graphed in Figure 2.2 is the relentless growth and decline of age groups as cohorts of differing size mature. The postwar baby boom (B in the figure) makes its first appearance in the 18–34 age group as that cohort reaches its growth peak in 1970–1975, moves on to the next elder group, and is finally reflected in the 1990–1995 increase projected for the 45–54 age class. The depression cohort (denoted D) passes through the life cycle preceding each baby boom peak, not surprisingly, by about 15 years.

Figure 2.2 shows substantial gains for the age cohort 35–44 in 1980–1995 and the 45–54 cohort in 1985–2000, periods when the increase of persons aged 18–34 drops off sharply and turns negative. The growing number of middle-aged persons raises one of the crucial questions about the future of housing: How can the market re-orient itself to the expanding clientele of this age group as the housing demand by young adults is reduced? Numerically, the growth of people 35–54 years old during the 1985–2000 period—over 26 million—will greatly exceed the decline in the number of young adults by 9.5 million. But this seemingly comforting statistic cannot be readily transformed into rosy projections of housing demand. The middle-aged are already housed, and they move far less frequently than their juniors, who are in the process of household formation and usually change from one housing unit to another before they settle in accommodations they consider permanent.

Nevertheless, the middle-aged do offer a potential for increased housing market transactions. A major thesis of this study, developed more fully as the analysis proceeds, argues that their market participation can be

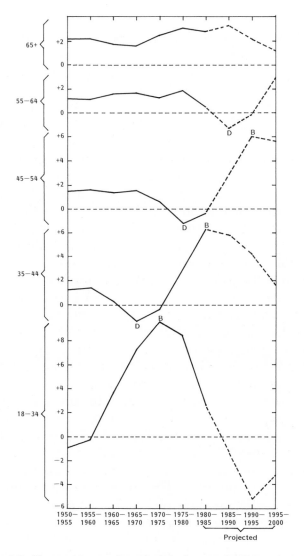

FIGURE 2.2. Changes in number of adults by age, by 5-year intervals, 1950–2000 (in millions); D = depression births and B = baby boom births (source: Table B.2).

activated by meeting their desire for dwellings of demonstrably higher quality in new construction and by quality improvements of existing housing as an alternative to moving. This prospect is enhanced by the income position of the middle-aged; they are at or near the peak of their lifetime earnings and as a group possess considerable discretionary spending power, part of which can be channeled into better-quality housing.

The age groups above 55 cannot be counted on to generate housing market transactions of much consequence. Despite the relocations associated with retirement, residential mobility declines sharply with higher age. Besides, the size of the 55–64 age cohort will not increase significantly before 1995. The growth of the elderly population (65 and over), at a peak in 1985–1990, will fall off sharply thereafter both in absolute numbers and relative to the total adult population. In both cases, the projections in Figure 2.2 reflect late echo effects of low births during the Great Depression and World War II, while the generation of the postwar baby boom will not yet reach the age encompassed in the senior groups.

Finally, there will be a considerable slowdown in the growth of the *total* adult population, the universe for our analysis of changing age distributions. In 1960–1980, adults increased by 48 million people. The projected increase between 1980 and the end of the century amounts to only 37 million, or three-quarters the number of the previous two decades. The decline results from the general retardation of population growth as well as shifts in age composition. It may also reflect an unduly low estimate of immigration by the Bureau of the Census. Nevertheless, it seems that the total demographic reservoir for housing market activity will suffer substantial shrinkage.

But the impact on housing demand of this shrinkage can and will be moderated as people change the ways of arranging themselves in households. As will be seen, households have grown at a much faster rate than population because the desire for separate living accommodations intensified and the capacity to pay for them improved. In fact, not only has the disparity between growth of population and households provided the major support for the housing market in the 1970s, but it will contribute to the market's vitality in the years ahead.

How reliable are the census projections of the population and its age distribution to the year 2000? Compared to other demographic and to economic projections, the estimates are on fairly solid ground. Even those reaching age 18–34 between now and the turn of the century are already born, so no guesses are necessary for births in the intervening period. Among the assumptions underlying the projections, future net immigration is the only one that raises questions. This component of population growth and other assumptions are summarized in Appendix A.

SLOWING GROWTH OF HOUSEHOLDS

While the projected decline in the generation of young adults can be viewed as a purely demographic phenomenon, household formation depends on both economic and demographic forces. This is certainly true for the short run. Under adverse business conditions, for example, marriage may be postponed or young couples may live temporarily with parents. Increasing numbers of single adults and one-parent families are unable to afford a separate dwelling unit, sharing instead their housing accommodation with relatives or others in already established households.

Economic factors can also restrain or stimulate household formation in the long run. Consumer preferences for separate living arrangements constitute a necessary but not a sufficient condition for the growth of households. Individuals and groups other than married couples, in particular, are in a better position to pay for a housing unit of their own when real incomes are rising at a rapid rate or the real user cost of housing services declines. The long-term trend toward greater labor force participation by women, though not wholly determined by economic forces, rests on the availability of jobs. In an earlier era, the change from the extended family (which included some of the householder's relatives such as a parent or in-law and a single uncle or aunt) to the nuclear family so common today was greatly facilitated by rising prosperity.

In the 1950–1980 period, demographic and economic trends combined to favor increasing household formation. The number of households rose by nearly 82% from 43.5 million to 79 million. The average of 2.7% per year was double the annual rate between 1980 and 1984. It has often been noted that household growth exceeded the growth of the total population, which was 49% or 1.6 percent per year. It also exceeded by a large margin the 56% increase of the adult population (18 years or more) that represents the reservoir for household formation.[2] The difference between the two sets of data reflects, of course, the inclusion of children and adolescents in the total population. The main point of the statistics is that by 1980 nearly one of every two adults was a household head.

Turning to projections for households, these are more tenuous than the projections of the adult population presented at the beginning of this chapter. Among other things, they require estimates of marital status, which are influenced by future marriages and divorces, and of the ways that people who are not married will arrange their living accommodations. As was indicated, changes of this kind depend partly on economic conditions. The Census Bureau makes no explicit economic assumptions for its various series of household projections. Instead, it extrapolates previous trends in marital status and in household formation by groups other than married couples. Extrapolations can differ depending on the period selected as a base, and on projections of population by age and sex. Economic conditions are implicit in the choice of the base period.

Household projections are especially tenuous at present. Census estimates issued in 1979 turned out to miss the mark for 1980–1984. A new illustrative set was issued as this volume went to press and could therefore not be used. Hence, the data presented here show a high 1979 projection (census series B) and a low (series D), together with averages of the two that seem more trustworthy than either. The following discussion refers to the averages unless indicated otherwise. The results differ from the illustrative set in detail, for instance, for household composition, but not for the broad trend changes.[3]

According to the time series in Figure 2.3 and Table 2.1, the future will fail to replicate the rapid growth of households that characterized the 1960s and 1970s. The 5-year increase of households in 1975–1980 represents a peak, followed by sharp successive declines to 1990–1995. In this last period, household formation would be just

TABLE 2.1. Number and Average Size of Households,
Actual and Projected, by 5-Year Intervals,
1950–1995 (Numbers in Thousands)[a,b]

Year	Number	Increase		Persons per household
		Number	Percent	
		Actual		
1950	43,554	—	—	3.37
1955	47,874	4320	9.9%	3.33
1960	52,799	4925	10.3	3.33
1965	57,436	4637	8.8	3.29
1970	63,401	5965	10.4	3.14
1975	71,163	7762	12.2	2.94
1980	80,776	9613	13.5	2.76
		Projection D		
1985	87,947	7171	8.9	2.64
1990	94,056	6109	6.9	2.58
1995	98,928	4872	5.2	2.55
		Projection B		
1985	89,570	8794	10.9	2.58
1990	97,749	8179	9.1	2.47
1995	105,034	7285	7.5	2.39
		Average of D and B projections		
1985	88,759	7983	9.9	2.61
1990	95,902	7143	8.0	2.52
1995	101,980	6078	6.3	2.47

[a]The household projections do not extend beyond 1995.
[b]Source: U.S. Bureau of the Census (1979). The 1950–1980 data are as of March, projections as of July. Projected numbers of households have been adjusted for minor underestimation of the 1980 population by multiplying each estimate by the ratio of actual 1980 to estimated 1980.

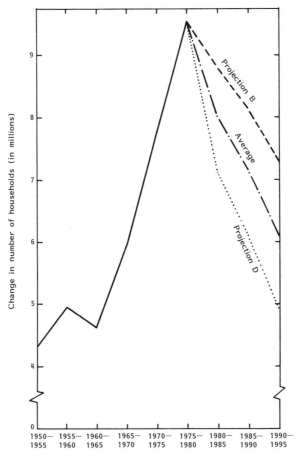

FIGURE 2.3. Five-year changes in number of households, actual 1950–1980 and alternative projections 1980–1995 (source: Table 2.1).

slightly above the level of 1965–1970 despite the large additions to the adult population in the interim. All of the estimates predict a substantial downward movement in the number of additional households but differ somewhat in its timing and magnitude.

The historic decline of average household size will continue no matter which one of the census projections is adopted. Any other forecast would involve a reversal of perhaps the best-established trend of the many analyzed in this volume. Ever since it has been measured, average household size has declined; its present level is half the size registered in 1850 (Seward, 1978). The estimated 1995 average is 2.47 persons, compared to 3.33 in 1960 and 2.69 in 1985.

The analysis of 1950–1980 trends emphasized that the growth of households exceeded that of not only the total population but also the adult population. Despite the projected slowdown of household formation, the same relationship would hold in the future. When series B and D are averaged, households would grow by 26% between 1980 and 1995, compared to an 18% increase in total population and a 22% gain in the number of adults.

THE FUTURE SHIFT TO MIDDLE-AGED HOUSEHOLD HEADS

The diminishing share of young adults in the future population will result in a higher proportion of households headed by older people.[4] This shift is of considerable importance to housing demand, for the young adults constituted a growing component of all households in the recent past and provided a strategic source of new household formation. Households headed by persons under 35 years of age represented nearly 31% of all householders in 1980 as against 23% in 1960. According to the projections, their share in the total will decline after 1985.

The relative importance of households headed by persons who are 35–54 years old, designated here as "middle-aged," shows an opposite pattern. These decreased between 1950 and 1980 but will grow substantially during the projection period. As the individuals born during the postwar baby boom enter middle age, large gains occur first among the 35–54 group of householders and then among the 45–54 age cohort. Other prospective changes in the age composition of householders are less significant for housing markets. Households headed by persons in the 55–64 age bracket will account for a decreasing portion of the total, and those headed by seniors (65 and over) will have a rather stable share.

The inventory data analyzed so far mask far greater periodic *changes* in the distribution of households by age of head. These are shown in Figure 2.4, where averages of the B and D projections are used. During the past three decades, additional householders in the young adult cohort rose from 1.1 million in the 1950s to 9 million in the 1970s, and their share in total household growth from 12% to as much as 52%. Under the projections, the numbers and proportions will decline precipitiously in the 1980s and become negative in the early 1990s.

The opposite trends for middle-aged householders again appear in sharp relief. In the historical period, the number of additional households headed by persons 35–54 years old shows a mixed pattern but their share in total household gains decreased markedly, reflecting echo effects of the low births during the Great Depression and World War II. In the projection period, the increments to middle-aged householders increase rapidly in num-

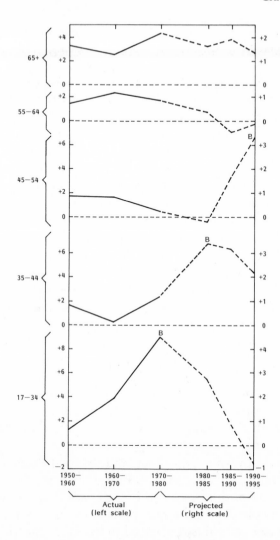

FIGURE 2.4. Changes in number of households by age of head, 1950–1995 (in millions); B = baby boom births (source: Table B.4).

ber and relative to total household growth, to the point where they account for over 90% of total 1990–1995 growth. It should be noted that the changes analyzed here represent shifts over time in the age distribution of householders and are not identical with *new* household formation. For example, Joe Doe, born in 1953 during the baby boom, married and establishing a household in 1975, appears as a householder in the under-35 group in 1980 but in the 35–44 group in 1990.

The prospective growth of additional households headed by the middle aged, together with the decline for young adults, presents a new challenge to those who furnish or influence the housing supply, including the alteration and modernization of existing dwellings. How can they retarget their market by stimulating the demand for higher-quality products and better locations on the part of a population segment that is already housed? The factors involved in this question are too numerous and complex to be considered here and will be examined in Chapter 5.

CHANGING COMPOSITION OF HOUSEHOLDS

The main driving force behind the increase of households relative to population during the past few decades was a remarkably uneven change in the growth of the various types of households. The family composed of a married couple with or without children, once the mainstay of household formation, has for some considerable time declined in relative importance. Less traditional groupings of people living in a housing unit have captured a rapidly rising share of all households. Before tracing this change, it is useful to specify the three types of households used in this study:

1. Married couples or husband–wife families.
2. Families headed by one spouse while the other is not part of the household, mostly one-parent families with children. Their statistical designation is "other families." Women predominate as household heads.
3. Nonfamily households typically headed by individuals. In this category, too, females outnumber males.

Some analysts combine the first two groups as "families" to examine contrasts with "nonfamilies." We prefer the above classification because the growth rates of the three types of households have differed markedly, and the housing implications vary a great deal. Individuals, for example, have more alternatives to living in a separate dwelling unit than do other groups. The same is true to a lesser extent for "other families" relative to married couples. Incidentally, unmarried persons of the opposite sex who occupy a common housing unit are included in the third category.[5]

Households of all three types grew during the historical period and are expected to continue their growth throughout the projection period. That is obvious from the data in Figure 2.5. Behind the aggregate numbers in the graph are remarkable compositional changes that have led to different distributions of households by type. For example, married couples accounted for only three

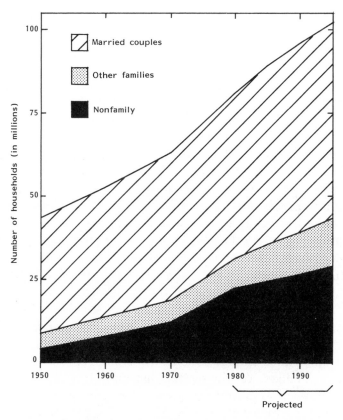

FIGURE 2.5. Number of households by type, 1950–1995 (source: Table B.5; projections are averages of the B and D census series).

households in five in 1980 as against four out of five three decades before; other families were nearly 13% of the total compared to 11%; and nonfamily households were 26% versus 11%. The greatest relative impetus for household growth has come from the last group as ever larger numbers of individuals sought the amenity of a separate housing unit. For every nonfamily household in 1950 there were nearly 4.4 in 1980. Also, the greatest compositional changes generally occurred in the 1970s. Other families, in particular, boosted their numbers and proportions substantially during that decade.

The shift away from the conjugal family as the traditional and major cornerstone of household formation emerges in sharp relief in the data for compositional *changes*. These, exhibited in Figure 2.6, show that the sources of household formation remained nearly constant in proportion throughout the 1950s and 1960s, then changed radically in the next decade. Increases in the number of married couples that contributed over half of total household gains in earlier decades accounted for only one-quarter in the 1970s. The growth of nontraditional households made up the difference.

The projections anticipate a further steady decline in the relative importance of married couples, compensated for by a growing proportion of nonfamily units, with only marginal fluctuations in the share represented by other families. Yet the overall distribution of changes in the projection period is a close approximation of those during the historical period. Married couples accounted for 40% of the growth in total households between 1950 and 1980 and are expected to account for 43% in 1980–1995; the corresponding figures are 15 and 19% for other families, and 45 and 38% for nonfamilies. Thus, the dramatic changes of the 1970s seem to be unique to that decade, with a return to "normalcy" in the years ahead.

Why should the drastic redistribution of household types in the 1970s virtually come to a halt? Do recent data

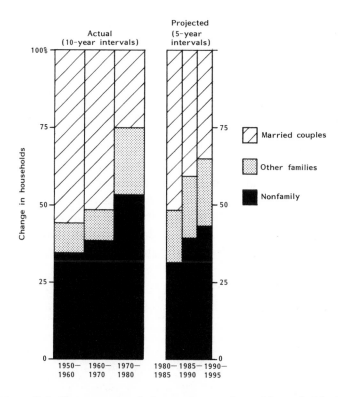

FIGURE 2.6. Components of change in number of households by type, 1950–1995 (source: Table B.6; projections are averages of the B and D census series).

on marriage and divorce, for example, presage a ''new era''? More broadly, are there indications that the socioeconomic factors determining household formation between 1950 and 1980 will change significantly? These are among the questions addressed in the next chapter.

APPENDIX A: TECHNICAL DETAIL
ON THE CENSUS POPULATION PROJECTIONS[6]

The projections use the cohort-component method in which the components of population change (births, deaths, and net immigration) are projected separately for each birth cohort. The starting point is the estimated population on July 1, 1982. This base is carried forward year by year by using projected survival rates and net immigration. Each year a new birth cohort of persons under age 1 is added to the population by applying projected fertility rates to the female population. All underlying data are age-, sex-, and race-specific. The principal assumptions of each series are as follows:

Subject	Series		
	Low	Middle	High
Ultimate lifetime births per woman	1.6	1.9	2.3
Mortality (Life expectancy at birth)	85.9	81.0	77.4
Yearly net immigration ($\times$ 1000)	250.0	450.0	750.0

The fertility rate in the middle series is consistent with recent experience. Life expectancy is projected to increase in all three series; i.e., mortality is expected to decline, as it has in the past. While the magnitude of changes in these two items appears well founded, the assumed volume of net immigration calls for comment limited here to the middle series.

First, the difference between gross and net immigration is quite small; annual outmigration is estimated at only 36,000 (U.S. Bureau of the Census, 1984, Table R). Hence, projected yearly gross immigration would be 486,000. This figure is consistent with the annual average of 491,000 in 1976–1980 for all immigrants including refugees. However, it ignores illegal immigration mainly from Mexico and other Central American countries. According to the Census Bureau, "because postcensal estimates do not include net illegal immigration, it was also necessary to assume that net illegal immigration is small." This assumption flies in the face of simple observation. On the other hand, no data are available on the number of illegal entries. In each of the past few years, nearly one million "deportable aliens were located" because they entered the United States without inspection (Warren and Passel, 1983). But the number of deported persons cannot be equated with the number of illegal immigrants. Some of the latter manage to escape detection. Also, many of them returned to this country shortly after they were apprehended and deported; i.e., deportations within a given year involve some double-counting.

Estimates of the number of illegal alien residents vary widely, up to 6 million, and they give no clue to the year in which they entered. A recent analysis by two staff members of the Census Bureau indicated a minimum of 2 million illegal aliens counted in the 1980 census. Of these, 890,000 were estimated to have entered the United States in 1975–1980, or an annual average of 174,000, but this figure merely denotes those illegal aliens who were included in the census count.[7] Others, fearful of any contact with officialdom, succeed in evading the census net. If 60% of illegal aliens were 15–34 years old, as the same analysis claims, the understatement of the population projections affects mainly the young adult group.

Under the circumstances, one can only acknowledge that the virtual omission of illegal immigrants injects a margin of error into both the historical and the projected population data. The errors are not huge. For example, if the official number of legal immigrants is doubled to 900,000 to take account of illegal entrants who remain in this country (instead of coming and going), the projected adult population is understated by 1% in 1985, rising steadily to 4% in the year 2000. If 300,000 of the additional 450,000 are young adults, the projected numbers of people in this age group are understated in a range between 2% in 1985 and 10% in 2000.

Finally, how much of the "middle-series" projections used here vary from those of the lowest or highest census series? As Table A.1 indicates, the variations for the projection period to the year 2000 are relatively small. For the various age groups, the lowest series shows differences from the middle series ranging from 0.7 to 3.8 percent. The differences for the highest series are of the same relative magnitude. The main findings of this study would stand if either of the extreme series were used. Throughout, the differences are greater for the year 2000 than for 1990. Indeed, the choice of census series becomes critical only when the projection period (ending in 2080 in the census report) is extended beyond the turn of the century.

TABLE A.1. Differences between Middle, Lowest, and
Highest Census Projections of Population, and
Benchmark 1980 Data (Numbers in Thousands)[a]

Year	Census series			% difference from middle	
	Middle	Lowest	Highest	Lowest	Highest
Total adult					
1980	164,028	164,028	164,028	—	—
1990	185,320	183,723	187,451	− 0.9	+ 1.1
2000	200,566	196,205	206,575	− 2.2	+ 3.0
Age 18–34					
1980	67,940	67,940	67,940	—	—
1990	69,323	68,694	70,466	− 0.9	+ 1.6
2000	61,016	59,753	63,176	− 2.1	+ 3.5
Age 35–44					
1980	25,881	25,881	25,881	—	—
1990	37,847	37,540	38,229	− 0.8	+ 1.0
2000	43,743	42,972	45,128	− 1.8	+ 3.2
Age 45–64					
1980	44,493	44,493	44,493	—	—
1990	46,453	46,136	46,767	− 0.7	+ 0.7
2000	60,886	59,859	62,025	− 1.7	+ 1.9
Age 65 and over					
1980	25,714	25,714	25,714	—	—
1990	31,697	31,353	31,989	− 1.1	+ 0.9
2000	34,921	33,621	36,246	− 3.8	+ 3.8

[a]Source: U.S. Bureau of the Census (1984).

APPENDIX B: DETAILED DATA ON ADULT POPULATION AND HOUSEHOLDS

TABLE B.1. Adult Population of the United States, by Selected (Numbers in

Half decade	Total adult	Age 18–34		Age 35–44	
		Number	% of total	Number	% of total
1950	104,994	40,111	38.2	21,637	20.6
1955	110,197	39,251	35.6	22,912	20.8
1960	116,146	39,047	33.6	24,221	20.9
1965	124,572	42,758	34.3	24,447	19.6
1970	135,291	50,035	37.0	23,150	17.1
1975	148,804	59,476	40.0	22,831	15.3
1980	164,055	67,958	41.4	25,886	15.8
1985	175,791	70,527	40.1	32,004	18.2
1990	185,320	69,323	37.4	37,847	20.4
1995	192,426	64,222	33.4	41,997	21.8
2000	200,566	61,016	30.4	43,743	21.8

[a]Source: U.S. Bureau of the Census, Current Population Reports (1984). Projections are the middle series.

Age Groups, Actual Data 1950–1980 and Projections through 2000
Thousands)[a]

Age 45–54		Age 55–64		Age 65 and over	
Number	% of total	Number	% of total	Number	% of total
17,459	16.6	13,390	12.8	12,397	11.8
18,921	17.2	14,586	13.2	14,527	13.2
20,578	17.7	15,625	13.5	16,675	14.4
21,839	17.5	17,077	13.7	18,451	14.8
23,354	17.3	18,645	13.8	20,107	14.9
23,924	16.1	19,877	13.4	22,696	15.3
22,739	13.9	21,759	13.2	25,713	15.7
22,464	12.8	22,188	12.6	28,608	16.3
25,402	13.7	21,051	11.4	31,697	17.1
31,397	16.3	20,923	10.9	33,887	17.6
37,119	18.5	23,767	11.9	34,921	17.4

TABLE B.2. Changes in the Adult Population of the United States, by Selected Age Groups, Actual Data 1950–1980 and Projections through 2000 (Numbers in Thousands)[a]

Half decade	Total adults		Age 18–34		Age 35–44		Age 45–54		Age 55–64		Age 65 and over	
	Number	%	Number	%	Number	%	Number	%	Number	%	Number	%
1950–1955	5,203	4.9	−860	−2.1	1275	5.9	1462	8.4	1196	8.9	2130	17.2
1955–1960	5,951	5.4	−204	−0.5	1309	5.7	1657	8.8	1039	7.1	2148	14.8
1960–1965	8,424	7.2	3711	9.5	226	0.9	1261	6.1	1452	9.3	1776	10.7
1965–1970	10,719	8.6	7277	17.0	−1297	−5.3	1515	7.0	1568	9.2	1656	9.0
1970–1975	13,513	10.0	9441	18.9	−319	−1.4	570	2.4	1232	6.6	2589	12.9
1975–1980	15,251	10.2	8482	14.2	3055	13.4	−1185	−5.0	1882	9.5	3018	13.3
1980–1985	11,736	7.2	2569	3.8	6118	23.6	−275	−1.2	429	2.0	2895	11.2
1985–1990	9,529	5.4	−1204	−1.7	5843	18.3	2938	13.1	−1137	−5.1	3089	10.8
1990–1995	7,106	3.8	−5101	−7.4	4150	11.0	5995	23.6	−128	−0.6	2190	6.9
1995–2000	8,140	4.2	−3206	−5.0	1746	4.2	5722	18.2	2844	13.6	1034	3.1

[a]Source: U.S. Bureau of the Census, Current Population Reports (1984). Projections are the middle series.

TABLE B.3. Number of Households by Age of Head, Actual and Projected, Selected Years, 1950-1995 (Numbers in Thousands)^a

| | Total households | | By age of household head | | | | | | | | | |
| | | | 17-34 | | 35-44 | | 45-54 | | 55-64 | | 65 and over | |
Year	Number	%	Number	%	Number	%	Number	%	Number	%	Number	%
					Actual							
1950	43,554	100.0	11,020	25.3	9,930	22.8	8,798	20.2	7,186	16.5	6,620	15.2
1960	52,799	100.0	12,146	23.0	11,572	21.9	10,688	20.2	8,584	16.3	9,809	18.6
1970	63,401	100.0	16,041	25.3	11,793	18.6	12,363	19.5	10,841	17.1	12,363	19.5
1980	80,776	100.0	25,041	31.0	13,974	17.3	12,682	15.7	12,520	15.5	16,559	20.5
					Projection D							
1985	87,947	100.0	27,176	30.9	17,326	19.7	12,488	14.2	12,928	14.7	18,029	20.5
1990	94,056	100.0	27,464	29.2	20,316	21.6	14,108	15.0	12,416	13.2	19,752	21.0
1995	98,928	100.0	26,117	26.4	22,358	22.6	17,213	17.4	12,267	12.4	20,973	21.2
					Projection B							
1985	89,570	100.0	28,304	31.6	17,556	19.6	12,629	14.1	12,898	14.4	18,183	20.3
1990	97,749	100.0	29,716	30.4	20,918	21.4	14,467	14.8	12,414	12.7	20,234	20.7
1995	105,034	100.0	29,620	28.2	23,423	22.3	17,960	17.1	12,289	11.7	21,742	20.7
				Average of B and D projections								
1985	88,760	100.0	27,740	31.3	17,441	19.7	12,560	14.1	12,913	14.5	18,106	20.4
1990	95,902	100.0	28,590	29.9	20,617	21.5	14,287	14.9	12,415	12.9	19,993	20.8
1995	101,980	100.0	27,869	27.4	22,890	22.4	17,586	17.2	12,278	12.0	21,357	21.0

^{a}Source: U.S. Bureau of the Census (1979).

TABLE B.4. Components of Change in Number of Households, by Age of Household Head, 1950–1995 (Numbers in Thousands)ᵃ

Interval	Total households		Components, by age of head									
	Number	%	17-34		35-44		45-54		55-64		65 and over	
			Number	%	Number	%	Number	%	Number	%	Number	%
Actual												
1950–1960	9,245	100.0	1126	12.2	1642	17.8	1890	20.4	1398	15.1	3189	34.5
1960–1970	10,602	100.0	3894	36.7	221	2.1	1675	15.8	2257	21.3	2554	24.1
1970–1980	17,375	100.0	9000	51.7	2181	12.6	319	1.8	1679	9.7	4196	24.2
Projected: Average of B and D												
1980–1985	7,984	100.0	2699	33.8	3467	43.4	−122	−1.5	393	4.9	1547	19.4
1985–1990	7,142	100.0	850	11.9	3176	44.5	1727	24.2	−498	−7.0	1887	26.4
1990–1995	6,078	100.0	−721	−11.9	2273	37.4	3299	54.4	−137	−2.3	1364	22.4
Average annual totals												
Actual												
1950–1980	1,240	100.0	467	37.7	135	10.9	129	10.4	178	14.3	331	26.7
Projected												
1980–1995	1,414	100.0	189	13.3	594	42.0	327	23.1	−16	−1.1	320	22.6

ᵃSource: Table B.3.

TABLE B.5. Number of Households by Type, Actual and Projected, Selected Years, 1950–1995 (Numbers in Thousands)[a]

Year	Total households[b]		Married couples		Other families[c]		Nonfamily households	
	Number	%	Number	%	Number	%	Number	%
Actual								
1950	43,554	100.0	34,075	78.2	4,763	10.9	4,716	10.8
1960	52,799	100.0	39,254	74.3	5,650	10.7	7,895	14.9
1970	63,401	100.0	44,728	70.5	6,728	10.6	11,945	18.8
1980	80,776	100.0	49,112	60.8	10,438	12.9	21,226	26.3
Projection D								
1985	87,947	100.0	53,824	61.2	11,345	12.9	22,778	25.9
1990	94,056	100.0	56,998	60.6	12,415	13.2	24,643	26.2
1995	98,928	100.0	59,357	60.0	13,355	13.5	26,216	26.5
Projection B								
1985	89,570	100.0	52,667	58.8	12,182	13.6	24,721	27.6
1990	97,749	100.0	55,326	56.6	13,978	14.3	28,445	29.1
1995	105,034	100.0	57,244	54.5	15,650	14.9	32,140	30.6
Average of B and D projections								
1985	88,760	100.0	53,246	60.0	11,764	13.2	23,750	26.8
1990	95,902	100.0	56,162	58.5	13,197	13.8	26,544	27.7
1995	101,980	100.0	58,300	57.2	14,502	14.2	29,178	28.6

[a]Source: U.S. Bureau of the Census (1979); projected numbers of households have been adjusted for minor underestimation of the 1980 population; percent distribution unadjusted.
[b]Because of rounding, the distributions may not add precisely to the totals.
[c]Families headed by one spouse while the other is not part of the household.

TABLE B.6. Components of Change in Number of Households, by Type of Household, 1950–1995 (Numbers in Thousands)[a]

Interval	Total households		Components, by type of household					
			Married couples		Other families		Nonfamily households	
	Number	%	Number	%	Number	%	Number	%
Actual								
1950–1960	9,245	100.0	5179	56.0	887	9.6	3179	34.4
1960–1970	10,602	100.0	5474	51.6	1078	10.2	4050	38.2
1970–1980	17,375	100.0	4384	25.2	3710	21.4	9281	53.4
Projected: Average of B and D								
1980–1985	7,984	100.0	4134	51.8	1326	16.6	2524	31.6
1985–1990	7,142	100.0	2916	40.8	1433	20.1	2794	39.1
1990–1995	6,078	100.0	2138	35.2	1305	21.5	2634	43.3
Average annual totals								
Actual								
1950–1980	1,240	100.0	501	40.4	189	15.2	550	44.4
Projected								
1980–1995	1,414	100.0	613	43.3	271	19.2	530	37.5

[a]Source: Table B.5

NOTES

1. For a summary of these, see Apgar (1982).
2. Demographers extend the analysis of households relative to population to "headship rates," or the number of households per 100 people in specific age groups and types of households (see, for example, Smith *et al.*, 1984). Since this study focuses on the housing supply response to demographic changes rather than detailed investigation of these changes, and because household data translate more directly and less ambiguously into housing demand estimates, headship rates are not used here. Instead, a later section of this chapter, "Changing Composition of Households," deals directly with the growth of various household types, the phenomenon statistically captured in headship rates.
3. Thus, our projection of total households in 1995 comes to nearly 102 million as against 100.3 million reported in the U.S. Bureau of the Census's illustrative projections (1986), or 1.67% below ours. Our estimates of the increase in the number of households from 1980 to 1985 is 21.2 million (26.2%), compared to 19.5 million (24.2%) in the 1986 Census report. The estimated household size in 1995 is nearly identical—2.47 persons according to our calculations and 2.48 according to the illustrative projections. The greatest discrepancy is found in the projections of households types. The illustrative set shows a smaller number of married couples than ours and a larger number of nonfamily households. The erosion of the conjugal family would thus be greater than our data indicate. It may also be noted that the 1986 Census report extends household projections to the year 2000 and includes, for the first time, alternative estimates based on a "robust economy" and on a "moderately growing economy."
4. The Census Bureau recently changed the designation "head of household" to "householder." The change has no effect on the data presented here. We use the two terms interchangeably.
5. The growth of this modern substitute for marriage has contributed to the declining share of married couples in the increase of total households and the rising share of individuals. The Census Bureau has estimated unmarried couples at nearly 2 million in 1984, when married couples numbered 51 million (U.S. Bureau of the Census, 1985, Tables 53 and 54).
6. For a complete statement, see U.S. Bureau of the Census (1984).
7. Warren and Passel (1983); the paper, despite its title, deals with all illegal aliens as well as those from Mexico, who accounted for 45% of the 2 million.

REFERENCES

Apgar, W. C., Jr. (1982). Housing in the 1980s: A review of alternative fore-
    casts. Cambridge, MA: Joint Center for Urban Studies of MIT and Har-
    vard University. (Processed)
Seward, R. (1978). *The American family: A demographic history.* Beverly Hills:
    Sage.
Smith, L. B., Rosen, K. T., Markandya, A., and Pierre-Antoine, U. (1984).
    The demand for housing, household headship rates, and household for-
    mation: An international analysis. *Urban Studies, 21* (4), 407–414.
U.S. Bureau of the Census. (1979). *Population estimates and projections,* Current
    Population Reports, Series P-25, No. 805. Washington, D.C.: U.S. Govern-
    ment Printing Office.
U.S. Bureau of the Census. (1983). *Statistical abstract of the United States: 1982–
    83.* Washington, D.C.: U.S. Government Printing Office.
U.S. Bureau of the Census. (1984). *Projections of the population of the United States
    by age, sex, and race,* Current Population Reports, Series P-25, No. 952.
    Washington, D.C.: U.S. Government Printing Office.
U.S. Bureau of the Census. (1985). *Statistical abstract of the United States: 1985.*
    Washington, D.C.: U.S. Government Printing Office.
U.S. Bureau of the Census. (1986). *Projections of the Number of Households and
    Families: 1986 to 2000,* Current Population Reports, Series P-25, No. 986.
    Washington, D.C.: U.S. Government Printing Office.
Warren, R. and Passel, J. S. (1983). *Estimates of illegal aliens from Mexico counted
    in the 1980 census.* Paper presented at the Annual Meeting of the Popu-
    lation Association of America, Pittsburgh. (Processed)

3

Socioeconomic Trends Affecting
Household Formation

Some major changes in the life-style of Americans during the past generation have favored the demand for housing. The rising divorce rate has in many cases generated two separate households instead of one. The growing number of single women holding jobs has raised their capacity to pay for dwelling units of their own or to afford better units. Increasing numbers of married women who work outside the home have augmented family income and lifted the demand for higher-quality housing and for equipment that eases the burden of household management. The greater tendency of young single adults to move from the parents' home to independent living quarters has given a boost to household formation. Broadened coverage of welfare programs and rising payments have supplemented low incomes and increased the ability of the poor to form households and enter the housing market. These changes, combined

47

with the growing numbers of "never-married" persons
of marriageable age and the surge of "twosomes" living together without the formality of marriage, have
reduced the importance of the conjugal family among total households and, at the same time, increased housing demand.

What is good for housing, however, may not be
good for society. Some social commentators have indeed
deplored the life-style changes of the past generation because they see them as a threat to the traditional family
which they consider a bulwark of a viable nation. And
they attribute many of the social ills that beset contemporary society—the high crime rate, widespread drug
use, and the rising number of abortions, to name a
few—to the breakdown of the family. Coupled with this
view is an often negative attitude toward the growth of
married women working for pay. If they preserved their
"natural" role as guardians of the home and children,
social disorganization would be lessened.

This chapter will not enter the heated debate over
the desirability or social consequences of life-style
changes. Instead, it will address itself to the more mun-
dane task of tracing the effects of such changes on
household formation. It will also deal with the critical
question whether the socioeconomic trends observed
during the life-span of one generation—in this case, during the 1950–1980 period—are likely to continue, moderate, or accelerate, or reverse themselves.

A RATIONALE FOR DISCONTINUITY OF TRENDS

We begin the projection of socioeconomic trends
with an analysis of why past trends cannot be expected

to prevail in the future. The most systematic case for discontinuity has been developed by Easterlin (1980), who argues that the size of a generation—the number of persons born in a particular period—is a strategic determinant of its welfare and living arrangements. Large generations, like the one resulting from the postwar baby boom, are at a disadvantage in the labor market because of oversupply relative to demand. A large labor supply affects adversely the economic fortunes of young workers—their earnings, unemployment experience, and opportunities for advancement. Young adults postpone marriage. When they marry, large numbers of the wives go to work to supplement husbands' incomes. For this reason and because of the uncertain economic outlook, the birth rate drops. Marital strains develop because family income remains below expectations or the wife's job is difficult to reconcile with the care of children, so divorce becomes more frequent.

Small generations, like the one born during the Great Depression and reaching maturity in the 1950s, have a better position in an underpopulated labor market. There is no economic reason for postponing marriage, the need for wives to work outside the home is greatly lessened, the birth rate increases, and the incidence of divorce declines. The lifetime income of those entering the labor force should generally be higher than the earnings obtained by members of a large generation.

Easterlin's analysis can be extended to households other than married couples. Those headed by individuals should rise in proportion to all households when a generation is small and therefore prosperous, and fall when it is large and less fortunate. Likewise, the higher divorce rate among a large generation should raise the proportion of truncated families, notably one-person parents with children. A small generation's lower divorce rate should have the opposite effect.

In brief, Easterlin postulates a self-perpetuating cycle as large generations plant the seeds for small ones, and vice versa. This is a long cycle exceeding the duration of the more familiar business cycle. Since the latter also affects demographic variables such as marriage, divorce, and household formation, we prefer for the sake of clarity to view the swings between generations as changes in the direction or intensity of trends.

The main point is that the theory of generational shifts applies immediately to the determinants of future housing demand, for this country is now in the transition from a large generation—those born in the postwar baby boom—to a smaller generation reflecting the declining births of the 1960s and most of the 1970s. According to Easterlin, then, it would be mistaken to project the socioeconomic forces affecting household formation in 1950–1980 into the future. Indeed, he makes a case for "a gradual but increasingly noticeable reversal of recent developments..." (Easterlin, 1980, p. 135).

Later sections of this chapter will take issue with some particular conclusions drawn by Easterlin from his generational analysis, and the next chapter assesses the link between cohort size and income. At this point, one must note that the impact of socioeconomic changes associated with the transition from a large to a small generation depends on the quantitative difference between "large" and "small." It surely matters whether the size of the small generation succeeding a large one is reduced by 10% or 40%. The projected small generation comes closer to the former rate of decline than to the latter. As was noted in the introductory chapter, the average annual number of births in 1963–1983 was about 12% lower than that recorded for 1946–62. Reflecting the echo effects of this change, the number of young adults (18–34 years old), the strategic group for household formation, is projected to drop from 70.5 million in 1985 to 61 million in the year 2000, a reduction of nearly 14%.

Throughout his work, Easterlin interprets the declining number of births after the early 1960s as a ''baby bust'' and implies that their effects on the subsequent formation of households will also be of bust proportions.[1] This notion must be rejected. The average annual growth of households projected for 1980–1995 exceeds the comparable figure for 1950–1980, though it is below the level of the 1970s (Table B.4).

As an alternative or supplement to Easterlin's analysis, the issue of continuity or discontinuity of socioeconomic trends may be examined more informally. One can postulate that at least some of these trends are apt to reach limits and then proceed to review recent data for indications of trend changes. The rising birth rate since the late 1970s, for example, may be viewed as a reversal of the previous downward movement but one that is unlikely to reach the dimensions of the postwar baby boom, which was a deviation from a *secular* trend toward lower birth rates.

Similarly, one can hypothesize that the declining size of households, from an average of 3.4 persons in 1950 to 2.7 in 1985, cannot go on forever; married couples and others living together without marriage vows will still constitute a sizable proportion, if not the majority, of all households. To take a third case, the rapid growth of the female labor force, leading to a participation rate in 1985 of 54% as against 76% for males, is unlikely to continue at the recent pace. Despite women's "liberation" from the home, some wives will prefer their traditional role of bearing children and keeping house. Hence, female labor force participation will probably never equal the rate for males.

The case for altered socioeconomic trends can be bolstered by pointing up the new conservatism that seems to pervade American society and politics, discernible in attitudes toward the role of government, in social mores, and even in the taste for "modern" art. Should this tendency persist, the conjugal family would regain much of its old position as the commonly accepted mode of living. But we shall leave this speculative subject to others and turn to the more pragmatic study of specific socioeconomic forces that bear on household formation and the demand for housing. In this effort, we shall use elements of Easterlin's work as well as the method of searching for recent indicators of change.

THE "VITAL STATISTICS"

To start at the beginning, births have shown a recent increase in both number and rate that seems to reverse their downward trend from the early 1960s to 1976. Demographers have carried on a lively debate about this subject,[2] but it is yet unclear whether the new baby boomlet has initiated a trend of lasting significance (Figure 3.1). Whether it does or not, future changes will have limited impact on housing demand. Even a sustained increase of birth rates will not affect household formation during the rest of this century. It will rather impinge on the size of families and households and possibly on the

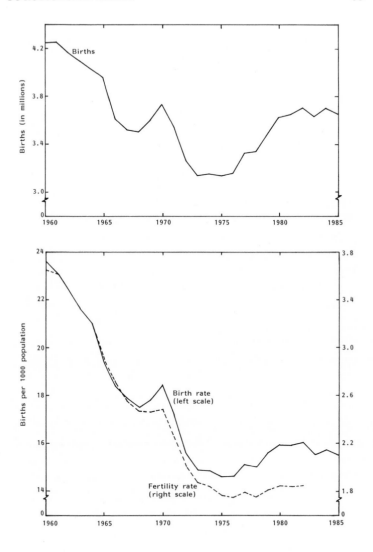

FIGURE 3.1. Births, birth rates, and fertility rates, 1960–1985 (source: U.S. Bureau of the Census, various years).

size of the dwelling units they require. It will also alter residential location preferences, for families with children generally seek housing accommodations in the suburbs and in reasonable proximity to schools, playgrounds, and other recreational facilities.

The quantitative effects of a sustained increase in birth rates on the sizes of households and dwellings and on residential location will depend on the parents' propensity for single or several children in the family. That choice, like so many described in this analysis, appears to vary over time rather than constitute a relentless trend in one direction. The postwar baby boom was characterized by a rapidly growing proportion of families with three or more children, from 14% in 1950 to more than 20% in 1960 and 1970 (and a subsequent drop to 11% in 1983). At the same time, the proportion of childless families declined but has recently reverted to its 1950 level of 50%. In 1982, 63% of women aged 20–24 and 37% of women aged 25–29 remained childless, up substantially from 50 and 29%, respectively, of women in those same age groups during the 1950s.

Part of the decline in fertility is explained by delayed childbearing, and part by the desire for fewer children. The cost of raising children is high and rising. One estimate puts it at $98,000 (in 1981 prices), much higher than an earlier estimate of $64,000 made in 1977 (Espenshade, 1984). In light of the greater public recognition of the high cost of raising children and educating them to the degree required in an increasingly complex society, it appears quite improbable that the pattern of the previous baby boom will reappear. More likely, a greater propensity for offspring will result in a rising share of families with one or perhaps two children.[3]

Although the fertility rate has fluctuated widely in the short term, it shows a negative secular trend. Except for the baby boom years roughly spanning 1947 to the early 1960s, fertility has decreased steadily since the beginning of the 19th century, when the average female bore about seven children. Viewed against the grand sweep of history, then, the baby boom rather than the recent decline is the aberration. While swings will surely continue in the future, the downward long-term trend in fertility seems firmly established.

At the other end of the life spectrum, people live longer. A person born today can expect to reach age 75, a dozen years more than a person born in 1940. The census projections of the population (Chapter 2) envisage a continued decline in mortality at a slow but steady rate. Increased longevity expands the number of households, but its more significant effect on housing demand comes from extending the retirement period. This tendency is reinforced by males' withdrawal from the labor force at an ever earlier age, as will be seen shortly.

With retirement periods and life expectancy lengthening, elderly homeowners are likely to increase their housing consumption for, when an investment earns returns over a longer time span, its attractiveness increases and the amount invested tends to rise. A prolonged state of retirement also often induces greater residential mobility in the search for housing suitable with respect to unit size, equipment, location, and even the type of structure, as exemplified by the large number of elderly who regularly follow the seasons in truly mobile homes.

Extended retirement will increasingly involve several successive housing decisions instead of just the one that is associated with the cessation of gainful employment. The decisions will in part depend on ambivalent attitudes toward full withdrawal from work; some retirees enjoy it while others opt for sporadic or part-time jobs. Whether the recent relaxation of compulsory retirement provisions will make a difference remains to be seen, but the evidence to date shows earlier retirement for males.

Within the time horizon of this study, marriage and divorce will exert a far more powerful influence on household formation and housing demand than birth and death. Perhaps the most stunning features of Figure 3.2 are the contrasting movements of marriage and divorce rates in recent years. The divorce rate doubled in the 11 years between 1965 and 1976 and continued to rise through 1979. Its stability in more recent years may reflect the severe business recession rather than denote the beginning of a new long-term trend. On the other hand, the marriage rate has declined sharply and almost without interruption since the early 1970s.[4] Divorces of late equaled nearly half the number of marriages as against a little over one-quarter in 1960. As one would expect, accelerated divorce has led to increased remarriages.[5] For the most part, however, remarriage merely means a game of musical chairs as far as the number of total households is concerned; a divorced person exchanges his or her dwelling unit for another, or the new marriage partner moves into the unit occupied by the previously divorced woman or man.

In contrast, the act of divorce, whatever it may do to people, may be a positive force in household formation. In many cases, both of the previous spouses retain or establish a dwelling unit of their own, so two households replace the one occupied by the dissolved

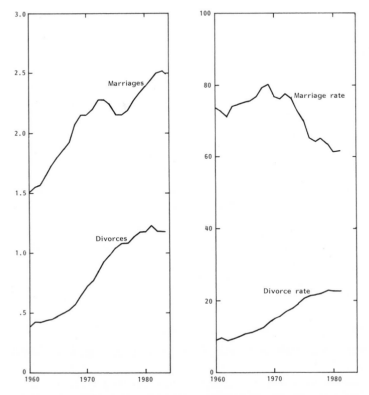

FIGURE 3.2. Marriages and divorces, 1960–1983; marriage rate per 1000 unmarried women, 15 years and older; divorce rate per 1000 married women, 15 years and older (source: U.S. Bureau of the Census, various years).

husband-wife team. On the other hand, both wife and husband may move in with families and friends, and one household disappears. The former is clearly the preferred alternative, especially for divorced spouses with children,[6] but hard times may force separated couples to opt for the latter. In an econometric analysis of the determinants of household formation, Hendershott and Smith (1984, Table 5.3) attempt to measure the impact of divorce. Although the divorce variable in their regression equations is not statistically significant, it is positive. The finding suggests that the net effect tends to be the creation of additional households. Its potential magnitude is illustrated by the following hypothetical calculation:

1. Women divorced in 1984   1.2 million
2. Assume that 90% of them stay in
   the unit occupied before the
   divorce   1.1 million
3. Assume that 40% of the ex-
   husbands move into a unit of
   their own   0.5 million
4. Sum of items 2 and 3   1.6 million
5. Net increase in occupied units
   (item 4 minus item 1)   400,000

As for the future, the number of marriages is apt to fall as the cohort of young adults, the main potential reservoir for new family formation, grows more slowly and then declines to the year 2000 (Chapter 2). The downward movement may be reinforced if the propensity for marriage diminishes, as it did in the past.

Two related statistics indicate a declining taste for marriage. For one thing, the number of unmarried couples living together has quadrupled since 1970, from about 500,000 to 2 million in 1984. Second, there has been a phenomenal increase in the number of never-married people in relevant age groups (Figure 3.3). The increase reflects in part a generational shift in social norms. It seems that getting married has all but disappeared from the list of life's "must-do's." As couples increasingly choose informal arrangements over exchanging marital vows, society has been growing increasingly indifferent to what, in a former day, was considered beyond the pale. Under previous standards both male and female homosexuals and those who were sexually ambivalent felt under some family or social pressure to

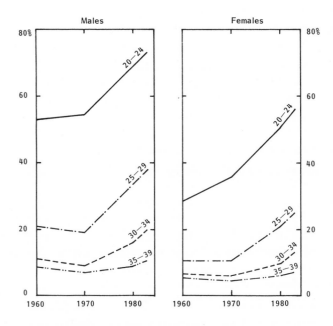

FIGURE 3.3. Number of never-married persons as a percent of total population in selected age groups, 1960, 1970, and 1983 (note: at higher ages the percentages tend to decline and the absolute numbers of never-married persons become quite small) (source: U.S. Bureau of the Census, 1985, Table 51).

marry. This pressure, too, has come to be relaxed. Hence, future marriage rates will be held down by the decision of growing numbers of people to stay single, giving a continued boost to the formation of one-person households.[7]

The current generation is less interested in getting married but, when they do, it is at a later age. Perhaps because of altered attitudes toward marrying and women's greater job opportunities, Americans are postponing marriage. In 1982 the median age for first marriage was 22.5 years for women, up from 20.3 a decade ago, and 25.2 for men, up from 22.7 years.

Of course, these trends may reverse themselves in the future but it is difficult to see why they would. The only prospect for change is offered by Easterlin's hypothesis of generational shifts. With smaller numbers of entrants into the labor force, workers would experience better conditions for jobs and advancement, develop greater confidence in their future, and be more inclined to marry or marry earlier.[8] Their average real wages would be higher than in the previous generation. Hence, greater purchasing power of young couples would in part offset the negative influence on household formation that results from their diminishing numbers. Whether such economic determinants will be sufficient to overcome what appear to be deep-seated social forces is questionable.

Turning to divorces, their number may decline in the years to come if only because most of them occur when couples are relatively young, and the population of young adults will diminish in the near future. As for the incidence of divorce, the rate per 1000 married women has already risen at a slightly slower pace since 1975 (see the changing slope of the rate in Figure 3.2) and even turned down in 1982, the first time in nearly 30 years. A reduction in the divorce rate would be consistent with Easterlin's theory of the effects of a generation's size on socioeconomic trends. It could indeed be part and parcel of a broader social change. The past increase in the divorce rate, one must recall, occurred at a time of growing doubts over the values of traditional institutions, rapid gains in jobs outside the home for women, widening use of contraceptives, broadening income supports for the poverty population, and greater popularity of feminism. These and similar forces that encourage divorce may well become less potent in the future. If so, a reversal of the divorce rate could have an unfavorable impact on housing. Just as the past acceleration of divorces probably added to household formation and housing demand, deceleration could have the opposite effect.

GROWTH OF WOMEN IN THE LABOR FORCE

The spectacular increase of women working outside the home—dubbed a "subtle revolution" by a writer on the subject (Smith, 1979)—ranks as one of the most remarkable of all recent socioeconomic trends. Many forces have contributed to this radical change.

Lower birth rates have lessened the conflict between child rearing and job holding. Even women with children of preschool or early school age who once required their mother's full attention can now resort to day-care centers or similar informal services, although many centers are too costly for low-income people. More and more elders who once were cared for in the family have moved to retirement or nursing homes. Labor-saving devices have eased the burden of household chores. The service sector, always a major employment source for females, has grown by leaps and bounds. Antidiscrimination rules have broadened career opportunities. The rising number of divorces has raised the proportion of one-parent households headed by females who are compelled to make a living in order to supplement (or substitute for) alimonies. Before its recent abatement, price inflation fostered labor force participation for maintaining consumption levels and, in particular, for sustaining desired housing consumption.

Women's earlier release from child-rearing obligations has also contributed to their greater participation in the labor force. A typical women born in the 1950s and currently in her 30s finishes rearing her last child at age 43. Her mother, if born in the 1920s, spent nearly 7 more years at this arduous task; it was not until she had reached age 50 that she was freed to seek paid work (Glick, 1977). Perhaps most important, married women have increasingly favored paid jobs over keeping house because they sought relief from monotony and social isolation or for the sake of the economic independence afforded by employment. Many have found paid work in the marketplace as the economically rational alternative to unpaid work at home, with the traditional housekeeping duties hired out to others. Better education and the feminist movement promoted a mentality that made work for pay not only a respectable but a wholly desirable alternative to women's traditional role.[9]

There are other advantages as well. Not only does a working wife's income lift the family's living standard, but it provides a cushion against financial disaster if the husband loses his job. A woman's sense of accomplishment and her self-esteem may get a boost once she enters the labor force. Her husband may be relieved of the sense of burden of being single-handedly responsible for the family's support.

Some negative points must also be recognized. Traditional power balances within families are upset. As time spent together grows scarcer, family life gets more complicated. Tensions arise when husbands believe that the wife's first job is still to run the house, even though she works full time. Parents may feel guilt-ridden over leaving their children in the care of a baby-sitter or child-care center. And some consequences are neither clearly advantageous nor disadvantageous. For example, a paycheck may give a wife enough financial independence to leave a shaky marriage; at the same time, a husband may feel fewer scruples about seeking a divorce when he knows that his wife can support herself.

To date, benefits of women working for pay have clearly been felt to outstrip the costs, as the statistical evidence shows. Moreover, surveys indicate increasing and widespread acceptance of womens' work. The National Opinion Research Center reported in 1983 that 77% of the men queried approved of wives working even when they had husbands who could support them, a figure that exceeded the 63% reported for 1972. The Gallup Organization, when it asked the same question in 1938, found only 19% of men approving of working wives. A Roper Organization pool taken in 1981 found that 29% of the men surveyed even preferred their wives to work, and only 25% wanted them to stay home (*Los Angeles Times*, 1984b, p. I-23).

The causal direction of changes in women's gainful employment is not always clear. Is the lower birth rate or the increasing "mechanization" of the household, for example, a cause or a consequence of women entering the labor market? Is the rising divorce rate a result of women's greater independence? In the context of this chapter, one need not resolve the chicken-and-egg puzzle but merely note the association and assess its importance. The effects of the growing labor force participation of females on housing demand, however, require some elaboration.

The paramount influence is that on household income. Married women who are gainfully employed add to family earnings; there has been a sharp increase in the proportion of married couples with multiple breadwinners. This condition promotes aspirations for better housing and facilitates upgrading through moving or capital improvements of already occupied dwellings. Single females, including divorcees and widows who work outside the home, are in a better position to establish or maintain households of their own or they can afford higher-quality housing. Thus, the rapidly growing female labor force in the past few decades has had a favorable influence on housing demand.

At the same time, the increase of married women at work has complicated the residential site choice. In bygone days, such decisions were mostly related to the husband's place of employment. Now, they often require a compromise between the needs of two breadwinners in the family who may work in very different locales. Episodic evidence indicates that the wife's choice of employer and type of work is more heavily influenced by proximity to the residence than is the husband's.

What is the likely future course of female labor? For perspective one must turn to the recent past, summarized in Figure 3.4. The work force participation rate of women has increased by two-thirds over the past three decades until today more women, whether single or married, are in the labor force than out of it. At the same time, the rates have dropped for males, a trend in large part explained by increased longevity, earlier retirement, and longer years of schooling. The converging trends in the chart tell the story of a remarkable assault on the labor market and one increasingly unaffected by the constraints that historically have excluded women from paid work. Participation rates for women with different family obligations showed great disparities in 1950. For example, only 12% of those with children worked compared to 41% of singles, who have a long record of working for pay. By 1985, however, the differences had all but vanished, with about half of women in all categories holding paid jobs. The only exception was the group of females with children aged 6–17 whose work participation has skyrocketed from under 30% to well over 60%.

Thus, the need for raising children is no longer seen as a great deterrent to the wife's working outside the home. The labor force participation rate of married women with children under 6 years of age in the household quadrupled in 1950–1982; and the rate doubled for those with children 6–17 years of age—more slowly because many housewives had always accepted paid work only when the youngest child entered school.

The increasing independence of women from child-rearing obligations is suggested by the changing age distribution of participation rates, particularly during the 1970s (Figure 3.5). As the data for 1950, 1960, and 1970

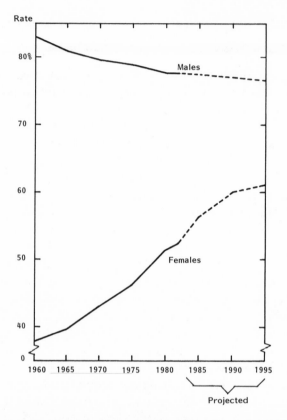

FIGURE 3.4. Civilian labor force participation of females and males, 5-year intervals, 1960–1995 (sources: U.S. Bureau of the Census, 1984, Table 671; U.S. Department of Labor, 1982, Appendix C, middle-growth scenario).

show, the rates dropped sharply for women reaching ages 25 to 34, then rose again. That dip has now completely disappeared, precisely at the ages when women customarily shouldered their child-rearing burdens. The remarkable change demonstrates how reduced fertility

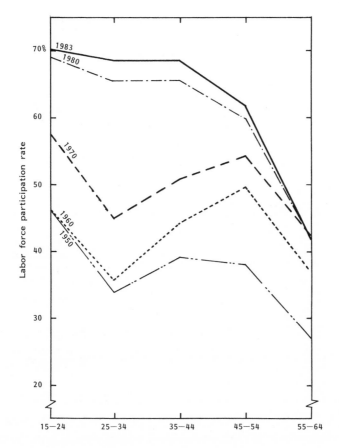

FIGURE 3.5. Female labor force participation, by age group, 1950–1983 (source: U.S. Bureau of the Census, various years).

and greater availability of alternatives to the mother's care have facilitated women's work outside the home.

How important is economic hardship as a force driving women into paid employment? Some observers argue that it is a prime cause for the extraordinary growth of married women drawn into the labor force. Easterlin's analysis is consistent with such a view; since the earnings of men in the large generation resulting from the postwar baby boom were relatively low, wives were compelled to seek paid jobs. There is no direct evidence on this point, but the data graphed in Figure 3.6 serve to illuminate it. The economic hardship hypothesis is supported by the observation that the families with unemployed husbands (the dashed line) show a larger percentage of working wives than those with employed husbands (the solid line). But the support is weakened by the fact that the difference between the two groups has not been large and has remained practically zero since 1980. For the long run, however, the findings suggest that economic necessity plays a modest role in drawing wives into jobs. Of course, the husband's unemployment is only one index of inadequate family earnings, but it is crucial.

The growth of women holding paid jobs has brought a rapid increase in the number and proportion of families with multiple earners, a trend that raises the demand for better housing. Two-earner families in 1984 accounted for 49% of all married couples with at least one member in the labor force as against 26% in 1960; thus the share of families enjoying dual incomes has nearly doubled. And the proportion of total families with three or more earners more than doubled in this period, reaching nearly 13% in 1983–1984.

The growth of female employment in the past few decades has been coupled with a notable trend toward better jobs. A few examples must suffice. Between 1960 and 1983, the proportion of females in "professional and technical" occupations (including schoolteachers) in-

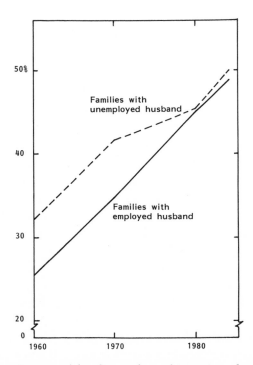

FIGURE 3.6. Percent of families with working wives, by husband's employment status, 1960–1984 (source: U.S. Bureau of the Census, 1985, Table 672; based on BLS and unpublished data).

creased from 36% of all employees in this category to nearly 48%. For "managers and administrators," the female proportion nearly doubled and the numbers tripled. Since 1972, the share of females has increased from 4 to 16% of all lawyers and judges, from 10 to 21% for "life and physical scientists," from 8 to 14% of physicians and dentists, from 28 to 36% for college and university teachers, and from 9 to 27% for engineering and science technicians (U.S. Bureau of the Census, various years).[10]

Between 1979 and 1985, the number of women employed as top executives at major U.S. companies tripled—from 8 to 29 (Lawrence, 1985, p. V-1). Time lags explain why the growth in female proportions in any job category may be high, while the proportions themselves remain low. The point is illustrated by another statistic: Females accounted for only 13% of practicing doctors in 1982, although one in four medical school graduates in that year were women (*Los Angeles Times*, 1984a, p. I-7).

Income gains associated with job upgrading are highlighted by the fact that nearly 6 million married women earned more than their husbands in 1981. These cases represented 12% of the married couples in the civilian population (U.S. Bureau of the Census, 1983).

Nevertheless, women's *median* earnings are still far below those of men. The female–male ratio for all workers stood at about 0.50 in recent years. This was an improvement over earlier ratios but still left an enormous gap. The ratios resemble (coincidentally?) those for adult females (30 shekels) to the values for adult males (50 shekels) assessed by the Lord and Moses, according to Leviticus (27:1–4) (Barrett, 1979, p. 34). For year-round full-time workers, the recent U.S. ratio has hovered around 0.60.[11]

The relatively low earnings of females are explained not only by sex discrimination but also by many other factors. One is the high proportion of part-time workers who in recent years constituted more than 1 in 5 employed women as against only 1 in 20 males. Much of the difference results from wives' responsibility for keeping house. Another reason for low earnings is the remaining concentration of females in low-paying jobs.[12]

Nearly two-thirds of all employed women do clerical and retail sales work as against only 1 male in 12. Further, large numbers of females have only recently entered the labor market and are not yet compensated for experience in their jobs. Finally, women interrupt their careers more frequently than do men.

Altogether, the income data provide a new perspective on the stimulation of housing demand through the increase of working women. When earnings are considered, the favorable effects on the housing market have been less marked than the mere growth in the number of working females would suggest.

A brighter future is in store, however, according to Smith and Ward (1984). By the year 2000, the disparity will have been reduced. Women's wages will be 75% of men's, a substantial narrowing of the present gap. According to the authors, women's wages rose appreciably after 1980. Real wages of black women have jumped 57% since 1956, and by 1984 the disparity between white and black women's wages had all but disappeared. Wages of young women aged 20–24 have reached a level only 14% below those of men the same age. Female workers' real purchasing power rose by 3.3% between 1980 and 1984 but dropped almost as much among males. Rather than government legislation, the underlying cause, the study contends, is the "closing experience gap" between the sexes, a factor that will continue to reduce the disparity in the future and increase women's purchasing power.

As was indicated earlier, it would be unreasonable to project the past growth rate of the female labor force into the future. There are already signs of slowing growth. The average annual increase of women in the work force was only 1 million in 1980–1983 as against 1.6 million in 1975–1980, and the corresponding yearly increase in the number of employed women was 0.6 million compared to 1.6 million. These figures—as well as others presented here—are unquestionably influenced by the business cycle,[13] but a declining growth trend to the year 1995 emerges also from the BLS projections shown in Figure 3.4. According to the numbers underlying the chart, the average annual increase of females in the labor force rises from 830,000 in the 1960s to 1.4 million in the 1970s, falls to 1.2 million in 1980–1985, to 1 million in 1985–1990, and to about 800,000 in 1990–1995. The spread between female and male participation rates will still continue to narrow, however, as the rate for males tends slowly downward while that for females keeps growing, though at a diminishing pace. In 1995, almost 90 females are projected to be in the work force for every 100 males, as against only 45 in 1960.

The BLS forecasts are as revealing for what they do not show as for the actual estimates. No reversal of the upward trend of the female work force is expected.[14] In other words, its growth is seen as a permanent social fixture rather than as an episode caused by the disadvantaged position of men in the past large-generation labor market, as Easterlin suggests. We concur in the BLS assessment. At the same time, it must be recognized that the slowing increase in the number of working women is beginning to reduce the added stimulus to housing demand from this source.

INCOME AS A DETERMINANT OF HOUSING DEMAND

That aggregate changes in consumer income exert considerable influence on household formation and housing demand is a generally accepted truism. Thus, income fluctuations associated with the busines cycle tend to raise or reduce the propensity for marriage and the establishment of single-person households. In the long run, the upward trend in real per capita income was a potent factor in the great improvement of the housing stock. But the positive effects of income gains on housing demand have varied in the decades since World War II. The number of households increased by 21% in the 1950s, about 20% in the 1960s, and nearly 25% in the next decade (Chapter 2). The substantial growth during the 1970s occurred despite a drop in real per household income. The data, reflecting the sluggish economic performance of the 1970s, *seem* to be inconsistent with the conventional assumption of income effects on household formation.

In fact, they are not. The surge of household formation in the 1970s in the face of declines in real income merely means that the favorable demographic forces were strong enough to overcome the negative income effects. Figure 3.7 illustrates the point. During the 1950s, the growth of real per household income accounted for 64% of the growth of total consumer purchasing power, the reservoir from which households draw for expenditures on housing and other goods and services; the increase in the number of households accounted for the remainder. In the 1960s, the importance of the two determinants was about equal. But during the 1970s the growth of households generated the purchasing power increment in its entirety. In fact, if real per household income had not declined between 1970 and 1980, purchasing power would have been 13% larger. (The dashed line in the chart, denoted $\Delta PP'$, shows the size of pur-

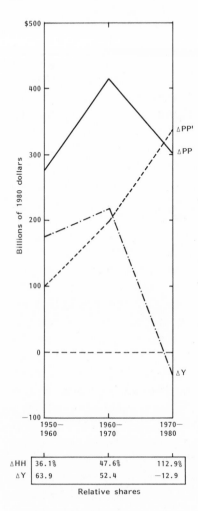

FIGURE 3.7. Contributions to growth of consumer purchasing power (ΔPP) by changes in number of households (ΔHH) and per household income (ΔY), by decades, 1950–1980 (source: Table D.1).

chasing power if incomes had remained unchanged; it is the equivalent of the contribution made solely by the change in numbers of households.)

In addition to the sharp increase of households, two other variables affecting housing demand, the growth of two-earner families and a decline in real user costs of housing, served to stimulate the market during the 1970s. Much of the nominal rise in family income can be attributed to the growth of multiple earners. The additional income, however, failed to translate directly into additional housing demand on a dollar-for-dollar basis due to imperfections in the credit mechanism. Because of fears that women's employment was only temporary, financial institutions have traditionally disregarded a wife's income in evaluating a loan applicant's creditworthiness or treated each dollar earned by a wife as less important than her husband's. Federal antidiscrimination legislation has attempted to remove this disparity. A 1974 amendment to the Civil Rights Act of 1968 prohibits sex-based discrimination in mortgage lending and requires that lenders take into account the couple's combined income. The Equal Credit Opportunity Act passed during the following year further prohibits discrimination based on either sex or marital status in transactions that involve obtaining or improving housing.[15]

Despite the new laws, however, Roistacher and Young (1979) discover from their examination of survey data that wives' current incomes are "discounted" either by lenders or by the households themselves, "suggesting that two-earner families have not exercised their full potential in housing markets." (Parenthetically, they also conclude, "Today's two-earner family may well be tomorrow's divorced couple.") It seems likely that discounting practices will decline in importance with more aggressive enforcement of the legislation on the books and continuing increases in women's job opportunities, work security, and labor market experience. If so, effective demand for housing would expand.

The second market demand factor, the real cost of housing services to consumers, dropped substantially during most of the 1970s (Figure 3.8). These findings from Hendershott's analysis are confirmed by other research. Van Order and Villani do not detect evidence of the much publicized "affordability" problem and conclude that "if anything, housing has become unreasonably cheap..." (1982, p. 101). Diamond (1980, Exhibit 4), estimates that the real after-tax average cost of homeownership declined by 20% between 1970 and 1978. The results may seem astonishing in light of growing local rent controls in response to public complaints over large increases in nominal rents, congressional proposals for federal assistance to first-time homebuyers, escalating house prices, and rapidly rising nominal mortgage interest rates—all parts of the housing scenario of the 1970s. The calculations of *real* user costs, however, go beneath the veneer of nominal prices and interest rates and, in the case of homeowners, take account of inflation gains and income-tax benefits.[16]

The reduction of the real user cost cushioned the effect of declining real income on housing demand in the 1970s. This condition, together with the strong demographic forces emanating from the maturing of the baby boom generation and the growth of multiple-earner households during the decade, suffices to explain the remarkable jump in household formation during the decade. It must be noted, however, that the real user cost of housing has been increasing in recent years.[17] Its future course is unpredictable. Under conditions of cost stability—an optimistic assumption—and in view of the

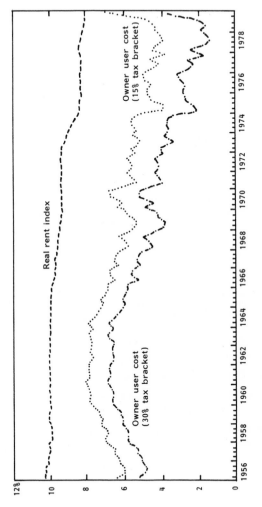

FIGURE 3.8 Real user costs for owner-occupied and rental housing, by quarters, 1956–1979 (source: Adapted from Hendershott, 1980, Figure 1; the data for the chart are given in Hendershott and Shilling, 1982, Table B, pp. 129–31).

weakening demographic base for housing, the market will more than ever depend on growing consumer purchasing power. Hence, Chapter 5 discusses the general economic climate likely to prevail through the rest of this century.

TRENDS IN THE ETHNIC POPULATION MIX

The analysis in previous chapters should have dissuaded the reader of the notion of a "typical" family or a "normal" household as the demand unit for housing. If such a notion was ever valid, it has long since been punctured by growing diversity of the persons and groups who occupy the dwelling units in the housing stock. Diversity has so far been expressed by highlighting the various types of households, the increased number of women holding jobs outside the home, and similar socioeconomic characteristics.

We now turn to yet another indicator of diversity, the racial-ethnic composition of the population. Because of cultural and earnings differences, the living arrangements of the so-called minorities vary a great deal from those of the majority. Over time, practically every variable affecting housing demand has been influenced by changes in the ethnic-racial population mix, and one must expect this influence to persist in the future. Hence, we conclude this chapter with a sketch of the most salient trends in the mix, without attempting a complete or even comprehensive treatment of the subject.

Tracing these trends is not easy, for it depends on the identification of ethnicity and race. Apart from inherent definitional problems,[18] the methods of identifying important minority groups have often changed from one census to the next. The figures in the Appendix tables must therefore be viewed as approximations. First, we record the growth of blacks, "other races," and Hispanics in the U.S. population.[19] This selection commends itself for the reason that data on the characteristics of households, families, and housing units are reported for the same groups. Blacks and people of other races accounted for 14% of the population in 1980 as against less than 11% in 1950, and their share in the total is estimated to reach nearly 17% in the year 2000 (U.S. Bureau of the Census, 1984a, Table H). The addition of Hispanics raises the 1980 proportion to 20.5% compared to 13% in 1960, the first year for which an estimate of Hispanics is available (Table C.1). Throughout, this group is probably underreported since unknown numbers of illegal immigrants from Mexico and other Latin American countries, afraid of contacts with officials, have managed to avoid population counts.

One of the noteworthy changes in the composition of minorities is the doubling in the number of people of "other races," mostly Asians, from 2.5 to 5.1 million persons in the 1970s. This growth rate by far exceeded that of either blacks or Hispanics. Even so, "other races" represented only 2.2% of the total population in 1980. Changes in the racial-ethnic mix are also apparent from immigration data. Newcomers from Asia and Latin America accounted for less than 6% of all regular immigrants in 1950 but nearly 80% in recent years. Those in the refugee category, a negligible number before the 1970s, have arrived for the most part from Asia. The proportion of Europeans and Canadians, the groups that fed U.S. population growth in an earlier era, has declined correspondingly. Similar shifts have occurred in the foreign-born population.

How do the demographic characteristics of the minorities and their living arrangements differ from the majority? Briefly, the disproportionate growth of blacks and Hispanics whose median age is far below that of the majority has augmented the younger segment of the U.S. population, adding to the number of adults at the stage of household formation. (It has also added to the supply of low-wage labor to do the ''dirty work'' shunned by whites.) Because of their higher birth rates, the minorities have also augmented the number of children in the U.S. population. The growth of blacks has contributed to the increasing share of truncated families in total households—families headed by a man and, more frequently, by a woman rather than by husband and wife. In contrast, Hispanics and Asians have maintained their strong conjugal family tradition. Reflecting largely their greater number of children, the size of minority families and households exceeds that of the majority by considerable margins.

Because of substantially lower income compared to whites, the above-average increase of the minority groups has kept up the demand for housing at the lower segment of the cost and quality range. For the same reason, and in the face of persistent though lessened exclusionary practices, the minorities show a much lower home-ownership rate than does the majority. In other words, their growth has reinforced the demand for rental accommodations. These and other characteristics are documented in Appendix C. One should note, however, that the housing conditions of the minorities have improved over time along with those of the population as a whole. Indicators of the improvement are also given in the appendix.

The absolute and relative growth of the minority population is apt to continue in the future, and so are the differential effects on housing demands. Higher birth rates alone assure further changes in the racial-ethnic mix of the population akin to those of the past. The shift toward a larger proportion of immigrants of non-European origin is likely to continue. On the other hand, the strong assimilative forces of American society will also persevere and raise the educational and occupational levels and, ultimately, the income levels of newcomers and especially their children.

Finally, the data in the appendix suggest that the minorities are not a monolithic group. On some criteria, interminority differentials are as large as minority-majority differentials. Thus, the conjugal family has remained the norm among Hispanics and Asians while it has been undermined among blacks and to some extent among Anglo whites. The educational achievements of Asian-origin students match or surpass those of whites. Median household income of Hispanics is substantially higher than that of blacks. Pluralism, an outstanding feature of our society, holds for members of the minority population as well as the majority. On balance, the past improvement of housing occupied by the minorities and the prospects for their economic as well as numerical growth suggest that their future increase will contribute to the demand for better-quality dwellings.

APPENDIX C: DATA ON THE CHANGING
ETHNIC-RACIAL POPULATION MIX

This appendix consists of two parts. The first presents detail on the demographic and related characteristics of minority groups that were summarized in the last section of Chapter 3. All data come from recent issues of the *Statistical Abstract of the United States*. The second part offers indicators of the housing conditions of minority groups compared with those of the general population. These draw on census reports.

Characteristics of Minority Groups

Lower Median Age. The minorities tend to be younger. The median age in 1980 was 23 years for Hispanics and 25 years for blacks as against 31 for whites. Similar differentials are reported for earlier periods. Without the disproportionate increase of these groups, the growth in the number of young adults, so important to household formation, would have been smaller. Future disproportionate increases will slow the decline of the young adult segment of the population.

Greater Fertility. The live birth rate per 1000 women aged 15–44 for blacks and other races exceeded the white race by over one-third in 1950–1970 and by 37% in 1980. The fertility rate for Hispanic women has also been higher than that of the general population. Since 1960, however, fertility has declined for all reported groups (Table C.2).

Different Household and Family Composition. Blacks show a strong and increasing contrast to whites. Married cou-

TABLE C.1. Blacks, People of "Other Races," and
Hispanics in the United States, by Decades, 1950–1980[a]

Category	1950	1960	1970	1980
		Thousands of persons		
Blacks	15,045	18,872	22,581	26,624
Other races	1,131	1,620	2,557	5,102
Hispanics	N/A[b]	3,465	9,000	14,800
Total	16,176[c]	23,957	34,138	46,526
		Percent of U.S. population		
Blacks	9.9%	10.5%	11.1%	11.8%
Other races	0.8	0.9	1.3	2.2
Hispanics	N/A	1.9	4.4	6.5
Total	10.7%[c]	13.3%	16.8%	20.5%

[a]For blacks and other races: *Statistical Abstract of the United States: 1985,* Table 29 (U.S. Bureau of the Census, 1985). "Other races" include American Indian, Eskimo, Aleut, Chinese, Filipino, Japanese, Asian Indian, Korean, Vietnamese, Hawaiian, Samoan, Guamanian, and "miscellaneous." The data for Hispanics are from the *Census of Population*; the 1960 figure is designated "white persons of Spanish surname" and may not be strictly comparable with 1970. The *Statistical Abstract* is the source for all data reported in this appendix.
[b]N/A = not available.
[c]Excludes Hispanics.

TABLE C.2. Birth Rate per 1000 Women
15–44 Years Old, by Decades, 1950–1980

Year	Blacks and other races	Whites	Excess of blacks and other races over whites (%)
1950	137.5	102.3	34.4
1960	153.6	113.2	35.7
1970	113.0	84.1	34.4
1980	88.6	64.7	36.9

ples among blacks constituted 60% of all households in 1960 and only 39% in 1983. The corresponding figures for whites were 76% and 62%, respectively. Among black households other than married couples, female heads predominate even more than among whites (Table C.3). Well over half of all black children under 18 were not living with two parents in 1980, as against less than one in seven of all white children. Hispanics and Asians, on the other hand, still show the traditional strength of the conjugal family, with 75% and 84%, respectively, of all households represented by married couples in 1980. Thus, housing demands of the different ethnic groups have varied a great deal and will continue to do so if past

TABLE C.3. Household and Family Composition of Blacks and Whites, 1960, 1970, and 1983 (Percent of All Households and All Families)

Year	Type	Households		Families[a]	
		Black	White	Black	White
1960	Married couples	60.3[b]	76.2	73.6[b]	88.7
	Other	39.7	23.8	26.4	11.3
	Male householder	11.0	6.8	41.0	2.6
	Female householder	28.7	17.0	22.4	8.7
1970	Married couples	53.3	72.5	68.0	88.7
	Other	46.7	27.5	32.0	11.3
	Male householder	12.0	7.8	3.7	2.3
	Female householder	34.7	19.7	28.3	9.0
1983	Married couples	39.1	61.8	53.4	84.7
	Other	60.9	38.2	46.6	15.3
	Male householder	15.9	13.5	4.7	3.1
	Female householder	45.0	24.7	41.9	12.2

[a]Excludes households headed by individuals.
[b]The 1960 figures are reported for blacks and other races and are therefore not strictly comparable with the data for later years.

trends are any guide. Household composition is one of the criteria of living arrangements that exhibit large interminority differentials.

Larger Families and Households. Black families are significantly larger than their white counterparts. In 1983 they averaged slightly over 3 persons each compared to 2.7 for whites. The contrast is still greater for husband-wife families. The differential has been reduced over time, however. The average size of black families exceeded that of whites by only 0.5 persons in 1980 as against 0.8 in 1960. Reflecting different birth rates and to some degree the acceptance of the extended family, households show a clear hierarchy of size descending from Hispanics to blacks to the general population (U.S. Bureau of the Census, 1980).

Median Number of Persons per Household

	1983		1970	
	Owners	Renters	Owners	Renters
Total population	2.5	2.0	3.0	2.3
Blacks	3.0	2.3	3.3	2.8
Spanish origin	3.6	3.0	4.0	3.3

Differentials in Labor Force Participation. Recent participation rates for black males were considerably lower than for white males, probably in response to discouragement caused by more widespread and prolonged unemployment. Black women, however, show higher rates than their white counterparts, and they are more likely to work full time. Differences are minor between Hispanic and white males as a whole, but the participation rate of Hispanic females is lower than that of all whites, perhaps because of their larger number of children or of persistent cultural resistance to wives seeking jobs outside the home (Table C.4). Here, as in other statistical comparisons of whites and Hispanics, one must note that the latter are for the most part included among whites.

Lower Income. Median household income exhibits a clear and consistent pattern: Hispanics rank second to all whites, and blacks rank third. The annual average income in 1970–1982 for Hispanics was 75% of that for all whites, and it was only 60% of the white average for blacks.[20] Year-to-year changes in these ratios were of minor magnitude. In view of the larger households of the two minority groups, per capita income differentials are even greater.

On the whole, the disproportionate growth of the minorities has tended to keep total household income and the demand for higher-quality housing at a lower level than would have been the case in its absence. In addition to the familiar determinants of income gaps between whites and blacks, the differentials of household income reflect the much larger proportion of households

TABLE C.4. Labor Force Participation Rates of Designated Population Groups, 1975 and 1983 (Persons 16 Years and Older)

Group	Males		Females	
	1975	1983	1975	1983
Whites	78.7%	77.1%	45.9%	52.7%
Blacks	71.9	70.6	49.4	54.2
Hispanics	78.8	79.8[a]	42.3	47.5[a]

[a]Data for 1981.

other than married couples and of those headed by females among the black population (see the subsection above on "different household and family composition"). Regardless of race, the pyramid of household incomes descends from husband-wife families to "broken" families headed by men and then to those headed by women.[21]

In the long run, however, the median wage or salary of individual black workers has risen relative to that of whites. Median earnings of black males in 1979 were 72% of white earnings as aginst 50% 30 years earlier. Black females working year-round and full time earned only 40% as much as their white counterparts in 1949, but the differential had disappeared by 1979 (Freeman, 1983, p. 126). The narrowing of the gap in personal earnings should continue with progress in the schooling and training of blacks.

Lower Rate of Home Ownership. Since household income has a potent influence on tenure, it is not astonishing to find that homeownership has been less common among the minorities than the general population. The ownership rate for blacks and "other races" increased from 35% in 1950 to 46% in 1983. The rate for whites rose from 57% to 68% in the same period. When the *number* of owners is considered, however, the relative growth of blacks and other races by far exceeded that of whites. In the 33-year period, the number of black homeowners advanced by 323% as against 121% for whites. Some part of this difference can be attributed to relative real income gains of blacks over the three decades, and part to the small base on which the percent is calculated.[22]

For Hispanics, reliable data are only available for 1970 and 1983; they show a marginal increase of the homeownership rate from 42% to 43% (U.S. Bureau of the Census, 1984b), in the same range as for blacks despite their superior median household income. The apparent inconsistency probably reflects the larger number of persons per Hispanic household and the resulting claims on its earnings for nonhousing expenditures. The per capita incomes of Spanish-origin and black households have been quite similar.

Differences in Housing Conditions

On practically all criteria reported below, the housing conditions of blacks are inferior to those of the general population. This is far less true for Hispanics. At the same time, both minorities have shared in the pervasive improvement of conditions since 1970. The evidence pertains to housing units. The complex data on neighborhood characteristics, reported along with those for dwelling units in the *Annual Housing Surveys,* are not included. These show inferior conditions for the two minorities and a mixed pattern of improvement and deterioration over time (for detail on blacks, see Grigsby and Hruby, 1985).

Concentration of Minorities in Older Housing Structures (Table C.5). The proportion of black households living in units standing over 20 years exceeds that of all households among homeowners as well as renters. It increased in the 1970s for black owner-occupants, as it did for all owners regardless of race or ethnicity. The proportion of Hispanic renters living in old structures was lower than

that of Hispanic or even all owners. The percentage of
Spanish-origin households in old rental housing also
dropped in the 1970s, as it did for all renters. There is
a notable contrast since 1970 between growing proportions of owners and declining proportions of tenants living in older structures across the board.

*Declining Incidence of Inadequate Plumbing Facilities (Table
C.6).* Despite pervasive improvement, housing units occupied by blacks in 1980 still showed a significantly
higher incidence of inadequate plumbing compared to
all units. The incidence for Hispanics was not much
different from that for the total occupied housing stock—
another case of strong interminority differences. On the

TABLE C.5. Percentage of Households Living in Residential
Structures over 20 Years Old, 1970 and 1980

	Owners		Renters	
Group	1970	1980	1970	1980
All households	48.1	54.6	62.1	59.5
Blacks	61.1	66.2	70.8	67.1
Hispanics	44.7	56.2	68.3	45.0

TABLE C.6. Percentage of Housing Units Lacking
Some or All Plumbing Facilities, 1970, 1980, and 1983

	Owner-occupied			Renter-occupied		
Group	1970	1980	1983	1970	1980	1983
All housing units	4.2	1.4	1.4	7.8	3.6	1.4
Units occupied by blacks	14.3	4.8	4.4	17.6	7.1	5.3
Units occupied by Hispanics	6.3	1.7	1.5	6.7	2.9	2.4

whole, inadequate plumbing is concentrated in rental housing, as are most of the other deficiencies.

Shared Kitchens and Bathrooms (Tables C.7 and C.8). The contrast on these two criteria is between blacks, on the one hand, and the general population and Hispanics, on the other. The incidence of shared or no facilities in housing units occupied by blacks was about twice that of all units in both 1970 and 1983, but it declined sharply in the interim period for blacks as well as whites.

Number of Rooms and Bedrooms (Tables C.9 and C.10). The median number of rooms per occupied dwelling has not varied much between blacks and the general population. On this criterion, it is the Hispanic group that shows a

TABLE C.7. Percentage of Housing Units with Shared Kitchens or Lacking Kitchens, 1970, 1980, and 1983

Group	Owner-occupied			Renter-occupied		
	1970	1980	1983	1970	1980	1983
All housing units	1.9	0.8	0	5.2	3.1	1.9
Units occupied by blacks	9.7	3.1	1.8	12.4	6.0	3.7
Units occupied by Hispanics	N/A	1.0	0.4	N/A	2.5	2.3

TABLE C.8. Percentage of Housing Units with Shared Bathrooms or No Bathrooms, 1970, 1980, and 1983

Group	Owner-occupied			Renter-occupied		
	1970	1980	1983	1970	1980	1983
All housing units	4.8	1.7	1.7	9.2	4.2	3.6
Units occupied by blacks	15.3	5.1	4.7	19.2	7.5	5.8
Units occupied by Hispanics	N/A	2.1	0	N/A	2.8	0.7

prevalence of smaller housing units despite larger families. The percentage of owner-occupied units with three or more bedrooms increased in 1970–1983 among the minorities as well as in the total housing stock, and at least two-thirds of the units had three or more bedrooms in 1983 regardless of occupants' ethnicity or race. The percentage was far smaller—one-fifth to one-fourth—in the rental sector. Here, black renters occupy a somewhat higher proportion of multiple-bedroom housing than either the general or the Hispanic population.

More Overcrowding in Minority-Occupied Housing Units. The incidence of overcrowding, measured on the generous standard of more than one person per room, exhibits

TABLE C.9. Median Number of Rooms per
Occupied Dwelling Unit, 1970, 1980, and 1983

Group	Owner-occupied			Renter-occupied		
	1970	1980	1983	1970	1980	1983
All housing units	5.6	6.8	5.8	4.0	4.0	4.0
Units occupied by blacks	5.5	5.7	5.7	4.0	4.1	4.1
Units occupied by Hispanics	5.2	5.4	5.4	3.9	3.9	4.0

TABLE C.10. Percentage of Housing Units with
Three or More Bedrooms, 1970, 1980, and 1983

Group	Owner-occupied			Renter-occupied		
	1970	1980	1983	1970	1980	1983
All housing units	64.8	69.1	68.7	22.8	22.0	23.1
Units occupied by blacks	59.8	68.7	69.4	24.5	25.2	24.7
Units occupied by Hispanics	59.3	68.6	67.0	20.5	20.8	20.4

a clear rank order: It is highest for Hispanics and lowest for the general population, with blacks in an intermediate position. Despite enormous progress during the decade of the 1970s, 12% of the Hispanic owner-occupied units, and 19% of their rented units, were overcrowded in 1983. Black housing shows only half this incidence. Overcrowding among the general population had become an altogether minor problem (Table C.11). The findings reflect, of course, the group differences in median household size and per capita household income. The pervasive reduction of overcrowding during the 1970s indicates at the same time that the constraints imposed by these two factors have been lessening, and they will do so in the future if fertility among the minorities continues to decline and income keeps rising at least at the modest rate of that decade.

TABLE C.11. Percentage of Housing Units with More Than One Person per Room, 1970, 1980, and 1983

Group	Owner-occupied			Renter-occupied		
	1970	1980	1983	1970	1980	1983
All housing units	6.7	3.1	2.3	10.8	6.2	5.6
Units occupied by blacks	16.3	7.9	5.7	22.5	10.0	9.0
Units occupied by Hispanics	22.9	15.7	12.0	27.9	21.8	19.1

APPENDIX D: CONTRIBUTIONS
TO CONSUMER PURCHASING POWER, 1950–1980

TABLE D.1. Contributions to Growth of Consumer Purchasing Power (ΔPP) by Changes in Number of "Households" (ΔHH) and Per Household Income (ΔY), by Decades, 1950–1980[a]

	1950	1960	1970	1980
HH[b]	49,295	56,537	67,714	87,442
Y[c]	$10,215	$13,796	$17,641	$17,074
PP (× 1,000)	$503,458	$779,984	$1,194,543	$1,492,985
ΔHH share[d]	—	$99,911	$197,173	$336,836
ΔY share	—	$176,525	$217,385	− $38,394
ΔPP (× 1000)[e]	—	$276,436	$414,558	$298,442

[a]U.S. Bureau of the Census, *Current Population Reports, Consumer Income*, Series P-60 (various).

[b]Lack of household income data before 1967 requires using the more traditional classification, families and unrelated individuals, to yield a complete time series extending back to 1950; overlapping and comparing results of calculations for households versus families and unrelated individuals during 1960–1970, when data for both groups were available, shows that the differences are minor and the major points stand as they are made in the text. For example, the median income of households in 1980 was only 4% above that of families and unrelated individuals, and the number of families and unrelated individuals outnumbered households by a margin of only 6%.

[c]Median, in constant 1980 dollars.

[d]Expressed as ΔPP′ in Figure 3.7.

[e]Contributions to ΔPP are calculated as follows:

For the ΔHH share: $Y_t(HH_t − HH_{t-10})$

For the ΔY share: $HH_{t-10} (Y_t − Y_{t-10})$

Their sum equals ΔPP.

NOTES

1. Technically, Easterlin's use of the term *baby bust* derives from his emphasis on birth *rates*, which are determined by population growth as well as the number of births. For the measurement of generational changes affecting household formation, trends in the number of births are far more relevant than those of birth rates. From 1960 to 1980, for example, the crude birth rate (per 1000 population) declined by nearly 32%, but the number of births decreased by only 15.5%.

2. See, among others, Sklar and Borkov (1975, 1976), Gibson (1977), Wachter (1975), and Wilkie (1981), and Bloom (1982).

3. The cost of raising children consists of direct out-of-pocket expenses and the opportunity cost to mothers of lost employment if they are or wish to be in the labor force. For estimates, see Reed and McIntosh (1977), and Espenshade (1977, 1980, 1984).

4. The significance of both marriage and divorce has recently been somewhat blunted by the growth of unmarried couples, i.e., persons of the opposite sex living in one household. These were reported to number 2 million in 1984 compared to over 50 million married couples, a ratio of about 4% (U.S. Bureau of the Census, 1985, Tables 53 and 54). The "twosomes" affect divorce statistics to the extent that their separation is not recorded. Yet they influence household formation in much the same way as do formal marriage and divorce.

5. The number of remarriages of divorcees and widows has nearly trebled from 197,000 in 1960. There were 51 remarriages per 100 first marriages in the early 1980s as against 30 in 1960. (U.S. Bureau of the Census, 1985, Table 120.).

6. Carliner (1975). At the lower end of the income scale, the program of aid for families with dependent children (AFDC) has enabled divorcees to maintain a separate household, keeping at least one dwelling unit occupied. Between 1960 and 1980, the number of families covered by AFDC increased from 0.8 million to 3.8 million, but, as a result of curtailments, the number declined to 3.7 million in 1984.

7. Beresford and Rivlin (1966, pp. 255–256) find a positive relationship between the income of young married men and the likelihood they will maintain separate households. Similarly, Michael *et al.* (1980) demonstrate that rising incomes generate demands for privacy and autonomy, hence the propensity to live alone.

8. Results of a recent survey suggest that changes in this direction may be in the offing. The American Council of Life Insurance found that 93% of baby boomers would "welcome more emphasis in society on traditional family ties" (Colvin, 1984, p. 30).

9. With respect to education, Easterlin (1980, pp. 65–66) presents data that refute the notion of reduced educational differences between the sexes, in terms of median years of school completed. But is it not the content and perceived objective of schooling rather than its duration that matters? Some decades ago, girls were educated mainly for their future role as housewives. Since that time, the curriculum and guiding spirit of their schooling have come to resemble more closely those offered to boys.

10. Because of reclassification of many occupations in official statistics during the 1970s, the percentages are approximations.

11. Median earnings from U.S. Bureau of the Census, *Current Population Reports, Consumer Income,* Series P-60, various issues.
12. For the data, see U.S. Bureau of the Census (1985), Table 699; see also Fuchs (1983), p. 135. Fuchs points out that working fewer hours leads to lower annual earnings even if the hourly wage for women is the same as for men. Further, wage rates are frequently lower for part-time workers because of fixed costs to the employer associated with each worker, regardless of the number of hours worked.
13. The past upward trend of women in the labor force or in actual employment has been so strong that cyclical fluctuations can be ignored for the purpose of this study. There was not a single year between 1950 and 1985 in which the number of females in the civilian work force declined, and the number of employed women dropped slightly in just two years (1954 and 1958). The data for 1980–1985 versus 1975–1980 are from U.S. Bureau of the Census (1985), Table 659.
14. Even the BLS's "low-growth" projections show a continuous increase of the female labor force, though at a slower rate than does the "middle-growth" scenario used in Figure 3.4.
15. For detail, see Roistacher and Young (1979).
16. In the case of Hendershott's calculations presented in Figure 3.8, real rents are calculated as the rent component of the consumer price index deflated by that index net of shelter; i.e., they are expressed relative to all other consumer prices. Real user cost of homeowners takes into account after-tax mortgage interest rates adjusted for inflation and the appreciation of owners' equity. Higher house prices generally mean larger mortgages, and those plus higher interest rates increase the advantage of tax deductions of interest payments of owners itemizing deductions. For detail, see the sources cited in Figure 3.8.
17. According to one estimate, the change in the real annual cost of owning a median-priced new home, negligible or negative between 1973 and 1979, rose in 1980–1983 by annual amounts varying between $2400 and $8600 (MIT–Harvard Joint Center for Urban Studies, n.d., Appendix Table IV).
18. These are illustrated by the tendency of some sociologists to extend ethnic criteria to the entire population, including WASPS, or white Anglo-Saxon Protestants. For a broad analysis of definitional problems, see Glazer and Moynihan (1975).
19. "Other races" in the 1980 census included American Indian, Eskimo, Aleut, Chinese, Filipino, Japanese, Asian Indian, Korean, Vietnamese, Hawaiian, Samoan, Guamanian, and a miscellaneous group. Hispanics present definitional and statistical problems. They include the descendants of the indigenous Mexican population in the Southwest that existed before the territory became part of the United States, as well as Hispanic

immigrants, mostly from Latin America. As the Census Bureau notes, they may be of any race. Besides, there is no acceptable estimate for 1950, and the data for later decades are based on varying identification methods and exclude an unknown proportion of illegal immigrants.

20. For Hispanics, the reference period is 1972–1982.
21. For all family households, the median income index in 1980 was as follows (husband-wife families = 100):

    Households headed by males   81
    Households headed by females   47

    Similar differentials are recorded in all annual statistics.
22. Median family income of black families, in constant dollars, rose by 88% between 1950 and 1963, compared to 81% for white families (U.S. Bureau of the Census, 1985, Table 743).

REFERENCES

Barrett, N. S. (1979). Women in the job market: Occupations, earnings, and career opportunities.'' In R. E. Smith (Ed.), *The subtle revolution: Women at work* (pp. 31–62). Washington D.C.: Urban Institute.

Beresford, J. C., and Rivlin, A. M. (1966). Privacy, poverty, and old age. *Demography, 3,* 247–58.

Bloom, D. (1982). What's happening to the age at first birth in the U.S.?—A study of recent cohorts. *Demography, 19* (3), 351–370.

Carliner, G. (1975). Determinants of household headship. *Journal of Marriage and the Family, 37* (1), 28–38.

Colvin, G. (1984). What the baby-boomers will buy next. *Fortune,* October 15.

Diamond, D. B., Jr. (1980). Taxes, inflation, speculation and the cost of homeownership. *Journal of the American Real Estate and Urban Economics Association, 8*(3), 281–298.

Easterlin, R. A. (1980). *Birth and fortune: The impact of numbers on personal welfare.* New York: Basic Books.

Espenshade, T. J. (1977). The value and cost of children. *Population Bulletin, 32* (1).

Espenshade. T. J. (1980). Raising a child can now cost $85,000. *Intercom, 8* (9).

Espenshade, T. (1984). *Investing in children: New estimates of parental expenditures.* Baltimore: Urban Institute Press.

Freeman, R. B. (1983). Public policy and employment discrimination in the United States. In N. Glazer and K. Young (Eds.), *Ethnic pluralism and public policy.* Lexington, MA: Lexington Books.

Fuchs, V. R. (1983). *How we live.* Cambridge, MA: Harvard University Press.

Gibson, C. (1977). The elusive rise in the American birth rate. *Science, 196*(April 29), 500–503.

Glazer, N. and Moynihan, D. P. (Eds.). (1975). *Ethnicity—Theory and experience.* Cambridge, MA: Harvard University Press.

Glick, P. (1977). Updating the life cycle of the family. *Journal of Marriage and the Family, 39*(1), 5–13.

Grigsby, J. E. III, and Hruby, M. L. (1985). A review of the status of black renters, 1970–1980. *Review of Black Political Economy, 13*(4), 77–91.

Hendershott, P. H. (1980). Real user costs and the demand for single-family housing. *Brookings papers on economic activity* (Vol.2). Washington, D.C.: Brookings Institution.

Hendershott, P. H. and Shilling, J. D. (1982). The economics of tenure choice, 1955–1979. In C. F. Sirmans (Ed.), *Research in real estate* (Vol. 1). Greenwich, CT: JAI Press.

Hendershott, P. H. and Smith, M. (1984). Household formations. Working Paper No. 1390 (June). Cambridge, MA: National Bureau of Economic Research.

Lawrence, J. F. (1985). New barriers block women on way to top. *Los Angeles Times.* September 15.

Los Angeles Times. (1984a). Female workers spur growth, create jobs. September 12.

Los Angeles Times. (1984b). Marriage: New freedom also spurs conflict over power. September 15.

Michael, R. T., Fuchs, V. R., and Scott, S. R. (1980). Changes in the propensity to live alone: 1950–1976. *Demography, 17*(1), 39–53.

MIT–Harvard Joint Center for Urban Studies. (n.d.). Home ownership and housing affordability in the U.S., 1963–1983. Cambridge, MA: Massachusetts Institute of Technology and Harvard University.

Reed, R. H., and McIntosh, S. (1977). Cost of children. Research Reports, *Commission on Population and the American Future* (Vol. 2) Washington, D.C.: U.S. Government Printing Office.

Roistacher, E. and Young, J. S. (1979). Two person families in the housing market. *Policy Studies Journal, 8*(2), 227–240.

Sklar, J. and Borkov, B. (1975). The American birth rate: Evidence of a coming rise. *Science, 189,* 693–700.

Sklar, J. and Borkov, B. (1976). Response to letter by Rosenberg. *Science, 191,* 424f.

Smith, J. P., and Ward, M. P. (1984). *Womens' wages and work in the twentieth century,* Report R-3119. Santa Monica, CA: Rand Corp.

Smith, R. E. (1979). *The subtle revolution: Women at work.* Washington, D.C.: Urban Institute.

U.S. Bureau of the Census. (various years). *Statistical abstract of the United States.* Washington, D.C.: U.S. Government Printing Office.

U.S. Bureau of the Census. (1983). Wives who earn more than their husbands. Special Demographic Analysis, CDC-80-9 (November). Washington, D.C.: U.S. Government Printing Office.

U.S. Bureau of the Census. (1984a). Projections of the population of the United States, by age, sex, and race, 1983 to 2080. *Current Population Reports*, Series P-25, No. 952. Washington, D.C.: U.S. Government Printing Office.

U.S. Bureau of the Census. (1984b). *Annual housing survey*. Washington, D.C.: U.S. Government Printing Office.

U.S. Bureau of the Census. (1985). *Statistical abstract of the United States: 1985.* Washington, D.C.: U.S. Government Printing Office.

U.S. Department of Labor. (1982). *Economic projections to 1990.* Bulletin 2121. Washington, D.C.: U.S. Government Printing Office.

Van Order, R., and Villani, K. (1982). Alternate measures of housing costs. In C. F. Sirmans (Ed.), *Research in real estate* (Vol. 1). Greenwich, CT: JAI Press.

Wachter, M. J. (1975). A Time Series Fertility Equation: The Potential for a Baby Boom in the 1980s. *International Economic Review*, 16(3), 609–24.

Westoff, C. F. (1978). Some speculations on the future of marriage and fertility. *Family Planning Perspectives*, March–April.

Wilkie, J. (1981). The trend toward delayed parenthood. *Journal of Marriage and the Family*, 43(3), 583–591.

4

Housing in People's Life Cycle

As the household passes through the various stages of its life cycle, housing needs, preferences, and capacity to pay change appreciably. To accommodate change, households typically move from one home to another or they make physical or functional alterations of the unit they occupy. With nearly one-sixth of the population now moving to a different address each year, the typical household may reside in as many as seven different places in the course of its life cycle between the ages of 25 and 70. The change may require not more than moving to a new place on the same street or the far more disruptive transfer from Cincinnati to Los Angeles. Long-distance relocation is often called for by job promotion or the search for a better job or, for many of the unemployed, a job pure and simple. Even in these cases, the life cycle plays an important role since relocation is unevenly distributed over the various age groups of the adult population, being concentrated among the young and middle-aged.

In any event, the exchange of one dwelling unit for another contributes the bulk of housing market transactions. Much of it is occasioned by changing requirements or preferences of consumers at different stages of their life cycle. Hence, this chapter attempts to segregate "the" housing market in a way held to be especially useful for demographic analysis of housing demand. It considers submarkets delineated by the occupants' age or, more precisely, by age groups of household heads. These submarkets reflect the preferences and economic constraints that determine the housing choices of households ordered by their age bracket. The result should be a continuous chronological assessment of changes in housing demands as the household passes through the stages of its life cycle.

This procedure merely represents a novel extension of the time-honored approach of dividing the housing market into a set of submarkets with different and often unique attributes so as to enhance our understanding of how the market operates. Regional and local markets, for example, are differentiated from each other as are the markets for owner- and renter-occupied housing. New construction and transactions within the stock of existing dwellings are segmented although the markets interact, and there are differences reflecting the size, quality, and location of housing units.

Each stage of people's life cycle involves crucial housing decisions that differ from those required at another stage—or differ sufficiently to warrant exploration. The new household formed by young adults must decide whether to rent or buy, where to locate, and how much housing it can afford. As children arrive, questions arise about the size of the housing unit and location or relocation close to services such as day-care centers and schools; the issue of homeownership and its financing becomes paramount. As children grow up and establish their own households, or with the parents' divorce, the family must decide between staying where they are or moving to another unit that better matches its altered circumstances. Meanwhile, as the household matures, income typically increases to a level that allows the upgrading of housing and its location. With the approach of retirement, new living options are pondered; the most important of these involves relocation in an area of lower living costs and greater amenities (even if it takes a cross-country move), and perhaps settling in a retirement community. The death of a spouse at the late stage of the cycle requires the survivor to weigh the merits of maintaining a separate household versus institutional living or moving in with the children.

To trace the housing choices made by adults in different age groups, the life cycle is here separated into intervals of about 10 years, with the following classification for household heads: 25–34, 35–44, 45–54, 55–64, and 65 and over.[1] Underlying the following analysis is the hypothesis that housing behavior is particular to an age group, with the age of the household head serving as proxy for life cycle stage. Just as higher-income families demand different types of accommodations than lower-income families, and small families require less housing than large, and households headed by females may have housing preferences varying from those headed by males, people also alter their housing in different phases of their life.

But if variations *between* age groups can be over-drawn in any snapshot of a population cross section, the temporal homogeneity *within* any age group can also be exaggerated. Because each cohort lives in a different era, it would be cavalier, if not erroneous, to ascribe the same behavior to any group merely because it is of the same age. For example, people in their late twenties and early thirties in 1980 were likely to differ in many respects from their counterparts in 1960. Most of the latter, born during the late 1920s and early 1930s, were raised with depression "mentalities" that persisted through later years. The 1980 group, on the other hand, was born into the postwar euphoria of a baby boom, and the optimism of that period shaped their attitudes and expectations.

Moreover, any age component of household heads in the 1970s is bound to differ from the same age component of the 1960s if only because household structure underwent such radical changes. These changes were quite unevenly distributed over the various age groups, as is evident in Figure 4.1. In fact, shifts in household structure turn out to be a function of the householder's age. The largest changes have taken place among the young adults, and their magnitude drops off with each later stage in the life cycle. It is the youngest who have most quickly seized the opportunities for adopting non-traditional life-styles. Each older group seems more resistant to the "social revolution" beginning in the 1960s. Ignoring this phenomenon would lead to projections of household composition by age that are far off the mark. Thus, while generalizations about the past are an inevitable ingredient of projections into the future, one must resist the temptation to graft the characteristics of one cohort onto future cohorts at similar life cycle stages.

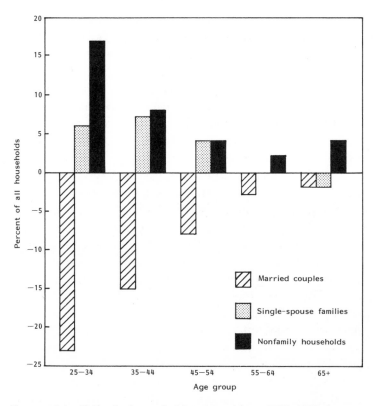

FIGURE 4.1. Shifts in household composition, 1970–1983 (source:
U.S. Bureau of the Census, *Annual Housing Survey*, 1970 and 1983).

STAGE I: ENTRY INTO THE HOUSING MARKET—
THE 25–34 AGE GROUP

Young adulthood is the period when most people
make the critical choices that will shape the direction of
their future lives. Major decisions are taken about work,

family and children, and housing. Occupational and geographical mobility are at their peak as people search for and settle on their first jobs and seek advancement. Partners are chosen, families are started, and nonfamily households are formed. Choices are likely to be corporate rather than purely individual, for the consequences of choices made by one family member diffuse to the others. Most marriages *and* divorces, for example, occur during young adulthood.

This life stage, together with the next age group (35–44), has been characterized by Fuchs as the "time to sow," for it is a period when households invest in their future. "The choices they make regarding work, migration, marriage, and fertility reflect in part their willingness and ability to incur current costs for future benefits—the wanting versus the waiting" (Fuchs, 1983, p. 26). The "time to sow" is literally expressed in child rearing. Nearly half of all families at this stage of the life cycle have children under age 12 living with them, a larger proportion than any other age class of families (Table E.1).

In addition to the human resource investments committed by people at this phase of their lives, households increasingly make the investment that, for most, ranks as the largest in their lifetimes: the purchase of a home. The average person enters the market for used houses at age 27, according to Rosen and Smith (1982, p. 29). Sixty-two percent of the married couples in this life stage were homeowners in 1983, as against 57% recorded in 1970, an increase that is especially noteworthy in light of the "affordability" issue raised during the latter part of the decade (*Annual Housing Surveys*, various years). The advancement from 1970 to 1983 may be partly explained by inflation, which added expected appreciation of house values to the prevailing consumption motives for home purchases. Another, more permanent, factor was the increased rate of female labor force participation in this age group, rising rapidly from 55% in 1975 to 69% in 1983 and projected by the U.S. Bureau of Labor Statistics to reach as much as 82% in 1995. The income of working women, whether married or not, adds to the financial resources available for homeownership. In any event, tenure choice ranks among the most important housing decisions made at this stage. Generational changes in life-style, real income, and expectations are highlighted by the fact that less than 40% of the married couples with households heads under 35 were homeowners in 1950, as against a sizable majority in recent years.

People typically form families before reaching age 25. More recently, the median age at first marriage hovered around 23 to 24 for men and 21 to 22 for women—a little higher than a generation ago—and the median age for first childbirth among married and unwed females has been remarkably constant at 22. But the proverbial ''7-year itch'' takes its toll. Divorce typically occurs at age 31 for males and about 29 for females (right on schedule, 7 years after first marriage). On average, divorcees remarry only 3 years later; for men, remarriage follows divorce after 4 years.

In view of the increase of divorce in the past few decades, young adulthood has indeed become a tumultuous period. Households in this age class have shown enormous compositional changes since 1970, evident in the following figures (U.S. Bureau of the Census, various years):

	1970	1980	1984
Married couples	82.1%	62.9%	58.9%
Single-spouse families	8.7	13.9	15.0
Nonfamily households	9.2	23.2	26.1

The increased share of single-spouse families reflects rising rates of divorce combined with falling marriage rates, but the rapid growth in the proportion of nonfamily households headed by individuals is even more remarkable.

During the 1970s, young households gave the housing market its leading edge because of the sheer size of the baby boom generation. Households headed by people 25–34 years old grew by over 7 million, an increment far larger than for any other age class. But the final impact on housing demand can only be appraised if the change in the group's real income is taken into account. The interaction between demographic and income variables will be investigated in the concluding section of this chapter for all age cohorts.

Meanwhile, the passage of time moves the baby boom generation relentlessly into middle age and beyond. The infants of 1946 will be 40 years old in 1986, well past the stage of entry into the housing market. Those born in 1960, the late phase of the baby boom, will reach that midlife age near the turn of the century.

STAGE II: THE YOUNG MIDDLE-AGED—35–44

Households at this stage of the life cycle are busily engaged in building careers and families. Concern with children becomes paramount. The share of the 35–44 age

group in all family households with children under 18—
38% in 1984—reaches a peak (Table E.1).

Housing decisions are greatly influenced by the additional space needs as children grow up. As will be seen shortly, they are also determined by increasing real income and a much higher rate of female labor force participation than in the past (which contributes to the income gains). The desire for homeownership intensifies and can be satisfied with improving capacity to pay. Slightly over 81% of the married couples in this age bracket were homeowners in 1983, compared to 62% for the 25–34 age group. On the other hand, young middle-aged households move less often than the young adults; in fact, residential mobility declines systematically with increasing age (Table E.2). Divorce is less frequent than in the turbulent stage of young adulthood, but recent shifts in household composition are still of impressive magnitude:

	1970	1980	1984
Married couples	82.1%	71.1%	67.2%
Single-spouse families	10.9	16.4	17.5
Nonfamily households	6.9	12.5	15.3

Numerically, the young middle-aged households are of particular interest because of their projected growth, as already indicated in Chapter 2. As the baby boom generation matures, households in this stage of the life cycle are expected to increase by almost 9 million, or 62%, between 1980 and 1995 (average of high and low projections). During the preceding 15-year period, 1965–1980, the number rose by only 14%. In 1995, they are estimated to account for 22% of all households, as against less than 18% in 1980. Moreover, the growth of households headed by the young middle-aged was greatest during the 5-year period 1980–1985 and tapers off thereafter. Nevertheless, their increase from 14 million in 1980 to a projected 23 million in 1995 is a positive factor for future housing markets.

The positive influence is reinforced by greater income. Households at this stage show the most significant income rise in the life cycle. Their average earnings were $118 in 1970 and $126 in 1980 for every $100 in the young adult group (Table E.3). Similar relationships were observed in earlier periods. In view of the projected numerical growth of these households, the income effects of their housing decisions on the residential market can be of substantial magnitude.

Female labor force participation in this age bracket is high and projected to increase. In 1983, the rate reached 69%, exceeded only by the 20–24 age group. According to the BLS estimates, it will surpass 80% in 1995.

Altogether, households at this life cycle stage show increasing stability, evidenced by reduced divorce rates, preponderance of homeownership, and lessened residential mobility in comparison with the young adult group. Stability becomes even more pronounced as households move into mature middle age.

STAGE III: THE MATURE MIDDLE-AGED—45–54

This is probably the most settled and stable phase of the entire life cycle. The position of the group in the world of work is more firmly established than that of any other. Relatively few of its members change their occupations, though they may move from one job to another. Whether they do or not, maturity is likely to mean advancement as a reward for experience or mere seniority. The divorce rate is much lower than in the two earlier life cycle stages. Deaths do not yet intervene in significant numbers to disrupt the family and confront the surviving spouse with major housing decisions. In line with other factors characterizing these households, the 1970–1984 changes in their composition are far less drastic than those for the previous age groups:

	1970	1980	1984
Married couples	77.1%	71.0%	69.4%
Single-spouse families	11.3	14.1	15.0
Nonfamily households	11.6	14.9	15.6

Only the "empty nest" syndrome begins to inject a new and dynamic element into living arrangements at this stage as grown children leave the parents' home to marry or to set up households of their own as single persons or as "twosomes." With the mother typically 22 years old at first childbirth, she is in her mid-forties when the offspring begin to move on. In 1984, only 15% of the family households had children under 18 living with them, as against 38% for the 35–44 age group.

Households at this stage generally are at the peak of lifetime earnings. Recent labor force participation rates approached 92% for males and 62% for females. Homeownership also reaches a peak. In 1983, over 87% of all married couples in the 45–64 age bracket (including those in the next stage of the life cycle) owned their homes.

The number of mature middle-aged households was quite constant at a little over 12 million in 1970–1980 and remained in this range through 1985. Only in the 1985–1995 period will the echo effects of the postwar baby boom reach this age group, with an increase to 17 million, or by 38%, within 10 years. The projected growth of households in combination with that for the 35–44 bracket can provide substantial support for housing market activity if suppliers find the means to stimulate the demand of the middle-aged for housing units more closely geared to their requirements in size and quality (see Chapter 5). The potential is reinforced by the high income of middle-aged households, which allows considerable discretionary spending, especially by those whose children have completed their education. Because many have fully retired their mortages at this stage of life, their major housing expenses are reduced to property taxes and upkeep. Besides, large numbers of the mature middle-aged have accumulated savings and own substantial amounts of financial assets. Ninety-one percent of all families in the 45–54 age class owned liquid assets in 1983 compared to 88% of all U.S. families, and the average value of holdings exceeded that of any other age group except families headed by persons 65 to 74, the age group registering the peak (Avery *et al.*, 1984).

The crucial issue is whether they can be induced to use their resources for upgraded housing. In the past, the decision to do so has been impeded by inertia, evidenced in low residential mobility rates, by the paucity of clearly superior alternatives in newly built dwellings, and by neighborhood ties. At least the first two of these factors are amenable to change. Besides, modernization of the dwellings already occupied by this group offers a considerable market potential for those who prefer to improve their housing *in situ* rather than by moving.

Others will be encouraged to trade up if tax laws continue to favor capital gains and allow indefinite deferral of such taxes as long as the proceeds from a sale are reinvested in another owner-occupied dwelling.

STAGE IV: THE SENIOR MIDDLE-AGED—55–64

In contrast to the two previous subclasses of middle-aged households, the senior group is expected to show no numerical growth through 1995. The baby boom generation will reach ages past 55 well beyond the projection period. Households headed by persons in this bracket will total a little over 12 million in 1990 and 1995, the same as in 1980.

The ravage of aging begins to take its toll at this stage of the life cycle. The death rate increases; in recent years, it was 18% per 1000 population as against 7 to 8% for the 45–54 group. Larger numbers of widowed spouses are facing the decision to stay in the family's housing unit or move into another or double up with grown children, remarriage at this stage of life being relatively rare. Labor force participation drops sharply, and the recent trend toward early retirement may reinforce the decline. According to the BLS projections, this trend will continue in the future but be concentrated among males. The participation rate for females is expected to remain stable over time at about 42–43%. In contrast, the rate for males is estimated to fall from 70% in 1985 to 65% in 1995. Median income of the senior middle-aged households is also considerably lower than that of the preceding age group—by as much as 14% in 1983. Because of the different trends in labor force participation, the income decline is concentrated among males while the income curve for females between ages 45 and 64 remains flat.

The falling income of this age class results from the increase in households headed by individuals as well as from early retirement or reliance on more sporadic work. The 1984 share of nonfamily units in total households, 16% for the 45–54 age group, was 25% for the senior middle-aged. The same pattern holds for 1970. The household composition of the 55–64 age class shows a high degree of stability, remarkable in light of the sizable changes noted for previous age cohorts:

	1970	1980	1984
Married couples	66.8%	66.0%	64.0%
Single-spouse families	10.5	10.4	11.0
Nonfamily households	22.6	23.6	25.0

A major asset of older households is the equity in their homes. The ownership rate of married couples, as was already mentioned in the previous section, peaks in the 45–64 age class. In many cases, owners in this group have repaid mortgages obtained for the original purchase, facilitating continued occupancy despite declining income. Households other than married couples headed by persons 45–64 also show a high incidence of homeownership. Sixty-four percent of the single-spouse families were homeowners in 1983, as against 31% for the same group with household heads under 45 years of age.[2] For single-person households, the 1983 proportion was 53, compared to half that rate for the younger age cohort.

The empty-nest syndrome affects the senior middle-aged families in full force. Four out of five family households in the 55–64 age group had no children under 18 living with them in 1983. The average size of household, already reduced from its peak of 3.6 for family heads of age 35–44 to 3.3 for those 45–54, shrinks further to 2.4 for the 55–64 group (U.S. Bureau of the Census, 1985). To what extent households adjust the size of their dwelling units downward as the number of their members is reduced is unknown.

The median number of rooms per unit in the housing stock has tended to increase since 1960 rather than decline, despite the shrinking number of persons per household over time. When families increase in size, homeowners in many cases can add or rearrange rooms to accommodate additional members, but the reverse process is far less common. More typically, renters as well as owners solve the space problem of family growth by moving. How they solve the problem of the declining family is impossible to document. Single-family houses are sometimes converted to two-family properties or landlords subdivide large apartments. Also, one suspects that condominiums and townhouses have recently played an as yet minor role in facilitating the adjustment.

Residential mobility is low, however, partly because job transfers in this age group are rare. Since the stage of senior middle-age is a transitional one as households are making plans for retirement, it is likely that major life-style changes, such as relocation, are postponed. The potential market for new, smaller, but better equipped housing units to meet the requirements of this group is probably thin and the prospect for major capital improvements of already occupied dwellings limited.

Stage V: The Elderly—Age 65 and Over

Whether the elderly population is viewed in terms of its current status or its changes over time, this group constitutes one of the truly distinctive housing submarkets. Given their astounding economic progress in recent years, theirs is a genuinely dynamic submarket as well. Measured in terms of relative growth rate, perhaps the most rapidly growing age-segment of the population is the most senior of the seniors: those who live to be 100 years of age or more. According to the Census Bureau, there were 32,000 people over 100 in 1980, or treble the number a decade earlier. Altogether, persons over 65 constitute one-fifth of all household heads and rank as one of the largest population segments.

The number of elderly households is expected to increase from 16 million in 1980 to 21 million in 1995, or by 30% as against nearly 40% during the previous 15 years, 1965–1980. Despite the public attention given to their past and projected growth, however, the *relative* size of the group is by far the most stable of all household age classes. Over the 1970–1995 period, the share of the elderly in total households varies by less than one percentage point from the 25-year average of 20.4% if the projections presented in Chapter 2 materialize. The only substantial increase occurred between 1970 and 1980. In the more distant past, the share of the elderly in aggregate households rose much faster, from a little over 15% in 1950 to almost 20% in 1970. In the future, the households headed by seniors are estimated to grow in tandem with the overall increase. Thus, the claim that American society will soon be awash in a sea of white hair is greatly overdrawn.

Changes during the past few decades have substantially altered the living arrangements and life-styles of the elderly, with significant consequences for the present and future of this housing submarket. Rapid income increases together with the growth in sheer numbers have reinforced their political clout. Sharply reduced labor force participation rates of elderly men and women, combined with greater longevity, have raised the number of years they live past retirement. Rising incomes and improved medical and home-care services have made it possible for more persons in the group to live with greater dignity and independently from their families by retaining their housing unit or moving to areas offering greater climatic amenities together with lower living costs. Despite this much publicized migration, however, residential mobility remains low. Elderly households, whether married or not, are the least mobile of all age brackets (Table E.2).[3]

Homeownership remains remarkably high despite the increased burden of "managing" it at advancing age and in the face of sharp reductions from the incomes obtained in the prime active stages of the life cycle. In 1983, for example, 86% of the married couples 65 years or older were homeowners, only a little less than the peak rate of about 87% for the 45–64 age group. Still more impressive, homeownership reaches a top rate for elderly households other than married couples, whether they be headed by males or females (U.S. Bureau of the Census, 1973 to 1983). Mortgages are probably paid off in most cases, and many localities offer partial property tax exemptions for the elderly of modest income.

Sex ratios that remain fairly well in balance through most of the life cycle go completely out of kilter with advancement into the last stage. One of the important characteristics of the elderly is the preponderance of female household heads among single-spouse families and single-person households. In 1983, the share of female heads in the two groups combined was 76%, reflecting, of course, the longer life of women. The household composition of the elderly is unique. Married couples account for considerably less than half of all households, and nonfamily units headed by individuals about match their share in the total:

	1970	1980	1984
Married couples	46.0%	44.9%	44.4%
Single-spouse families	11.7	9.6	9.7
Nonfamily households	42.2	45.5	45.9

As for income growth, the average elderly household fared better—and by a wide margin—than did any other age group during the 1970s. With real median income rising from $7409 to $8781, the typical household enjoyed a 19% increase. Mean household income rose from $11,475 to $12,628, a gain of 10%. The difference in rates suggests a pronounced narrowing of the distribution of incomes among the elderly.

The income increases resulted from the growth of pensions paid from private retirement funds, favorable returns on savings, and, perhaps most important, a benevolent public policy. The budgets for the federal government's commitments to retirement programs, including Medicare, are 4½ times the budgets for means-tested welfare programs (Longman, 1985, p. 73). Social Security alone will pay an estimated $182 billion in benefits during fiscal year 1986, an amount representing

4.4% of the GNP and a third of the federal government's budget for all nondefense programs (Feldstein, 1985, p. 102). Since the early 1970s, Social Security payments, which now reach over 9 out of 10 elderly and come to nearly 40 cents for every dollar of their income, have risen more rapidly than wages. The nonelderly, like it or not, are also contributing to the elderly's welfare, for the benefits of Social Security and Medicare are costing over three times as much as the current recipients' contributions.

The escalation of pensions and old-age benefits relative to wages makes retirement increasingly more attractive than work. The benefits–wage difference, together with the increased coverage by pensions and larger disability payments, helps to explain the growing numbers who retire early, with the average age for leaving work dropping from the traditional 65 to 62 (Mitchell and Fields, 1984). Even more striking is the declining proportion of people who continue to work into old age. In 1950 about one-half of all men kept on working past age 65. The proportion had fallen to fewer than one in six by 1984, and the Department of Labor projects a ratio of under one in eight by 1995.

The vast majority of the elderly hold financial assets, and for the nearly 9 out of 10 who do, the average amounts of such holdings are large and, not suprisingly, larger than for their juniors. In 1983, the mean total holdings of a family head 65–74 stood at over $65,000 (and $37,000 for those 75 years and over), or considerably more than twice the average for all families. The far lower median holdings of $11,400 (and $10,350 for the seniors over 75 years) indicate, however, that such assets were extremely unequally distributed (Avery *et al.*,

1984, p. 686). Nonetheless, the return on these holdings in many cases supplemented incomes from other sources such as annuities and other retirement benefits by sizeable amounts. Earnings on investments grew in the 1970s as interest rates on savings deposits and other assets were escalating, and they accounted for about one-quarter of the elderly's personal income in 1981 (U.S. Bureau of the Census, 1983, p. 9).

The income gains made it possible for increasing numbers of the elderly to maintain their own households and frequently to upgrade their housing status as well. Future increases in Social Security payments may be more moderate than in the recent past, but the political debates surrounding the 1984 presidential campaign left no doubt that a robust Social Security program, with payments growing at least as rapidly as inflation, enjoys strong bipartisan support and is very unlikely to be tampered with in the future.

The improvement of income over time has still left the elderly in a position inferior to that of most of their juniors. The median household in 1980 received an annual income only half that of all households (as against 40% in 1970) and amounting to only 45% of the income of those in the 55–64 age class. But the figures tell only part of the story. The clouds on the income position of those in their golden years have silver linings.

First, nearly one in three aged persons lived in poverty during 1959. Due to the factors outlined above, the proportion had dropped to 12.4% by 1984, two percentage points below the population as a whole. Second, money income fails to reflect the seniors' true economic position. Elderly persons increasingly receive cut rates for purchases ranging from bus rides, airplane flights, and groceries to movies, banking transactions, and public services. Seniors have benefited disproportionately from public housing, for not only are they among the few remaining groups eligible under sharply curtailed programs but they are regarded in most communities as "safe" and desirable tenants. Medicaid and Medicare have substantially eased the burdens of skyrocketing medical costs that plague the aged. Benefits received from these programs, plus food stamps, are not counted as income and many are not taxed. According to one estimate, when the market value of noncash benefits like food stamps, Medicare, and subsidized housing are counted, the proportion of elderly persons living below the poverty line plunges to 3.3% (Longman, 1985). Third, household costs are lower for there are fewer mouths to feed and tax rates reflect the reduced money incomes. In 1982, the average after-tax per capita income for households headed by seniors was $7845, more than $1000 above the average for all households headed by people under 65 ($6780). Fuchs concludes from recently published research that "the *after-tax* income *per household member* of the elderly is almost equal to that of the 45–64 age group" (Fuchs, 1984).

Nevertheless, the elderly who live independently must make difficult decisions to align housing consumption to reduced money income and the declining size of their households. The actions they have taken in the past have been marked by a great deal of understandable inertia. While much has been made of the growth of retirement communities, the share of the elderly choosing this mode of living must be small in view of their low general mobility. Also, the fact that most retirement projects have opened their gates for childless households of middle-aged working people is an interesting commentary on the limited market for housing strictly reserved for the aged. Condominiums and mobile homes have offered the elderly an increasing range of alternatives to conventional homes in recent years.[4]

Rising incomes have also offered the elderly a broader range of choices between independence and living with kin. Research by Michael *et al.* (1980) shows that income is a principal determinant of elderly widows' propensity to live alone. A review of the literature on the subject concludes that most elderly clearly prefer living by themselves rather than with their children and that the less favored alternative is chosen only when dictated by economic circumstances (Troll, 1971, p. 266). An increasing proportion of them have apparently been able to realize that ambition. In 1980, an estimated 18% of single women aged 65 and above resided with families of their kin, a sharp drop from 29% in 1970 (Shanas, 1980, pp. 9–15), and from 58% in 1950 (Glick, 1957, pp. 10–11). A continuing trend toward independent living should further increase the demand for one-bedroom and efficiency units.

The prospect for any substantial housing market activity generated by the aged depends on the capacity of builders to overcome the prevailing inertia of the group by offering products that more fully meet the special needs of the elderly and by developing marketing techniques addressed to this clientele. A special comment is in order, however, on two special aspects of housing occupied by seniors.

First, elderly homeowners are said to undermaintain their properties. According to Guttentag (1975), undermaintenance is perhaps the most widely used method of dissaving for elderly homeowners. There are at least three reasons: the lack of human and financial resources for good maintenance practice, the short life-span left for enjoying the return on upkeep and upgrading, and the location of many homes occupied by the aged in declining neighborhoods where property maintenance generally is poor. There is no easy remedy in sight. Most local efforts to organize renovation on a neighborhood scale have had little permanent effect, although they have often succeeded in the short run. Reverse mortgages or housing annuities under which older homeowners can transfer their title to a lending insitution at death in return for a current income may facilitate better maintenance but these instruments have so far been rarely used. Another innovation intended to reduce the burden of maintaining housing is the "circuit breaker." Some state and local governments permit certain elderly homeowners to postpone until death the payment of property taxes, but from a public policy perspective this method involves shifting the support of local services to the younger households and is therefore unlikely to meet with widespread public approval (Guttentag, 1975; Scholen and Chen, 1980). Moreover, many elderly are reluctant to leave their heirs an estate encumbered by tax liens.

Second, it has often been observed that the elderly are "overhoused," with reference to the proverbial widow who stays in the 7-room dwelling that once sheltered her whole family. Established neighborhood ties, apprehension over the chores of moving, and reluctance to double up with grown children (who may live in a different locality) are prime factors explaining their inertia. The general result is indeed a maldistribution of housing space. But it is difficult to see how market forces alone can improve a condition so deeply rooted in attitudes. The recent "granny flats" installed in the homes of grown children may signify greater acceptance of the old notion of the extended family. Whether this much discussed but still rarely used approach will become a significant solution of the dilemma remains to be seen.

HOUSEHOLDS, INCOMES, AGE, AND THE AFFORDABILITY ISSUE

The foregoing discussion of housing demand in different stages of people's life cycle suggests that the increase in the number of households and the change in real per household income have varied a great deal from one age group to another. The relationship between these two variables can now be specified more precisely for each age class, with the critical entry group furnishing a particularly dramatic example.

How much have household trends and income trends in the various age classes contributed to the growth of consumer purchasing power, the source of housing demand? The question is answered for the 1970s as an illustration of the valuable insights gained from such an analysis and in the context of the "affordability crisis," perhaps the most newsworthy housing complaint of potential entrants during the past decade, and one that still haunts the industry. Obviously, the data for one period cannot be simply projected into the future as age composition and the earnings of each age group change over time. Nevertheless, they are instructive as indications of altered relationships in the years to come.

During the 1970s, and particularly during the latter part of the decade, average house prices in many parts of the nation doubled in the space of only a few years (Grebler and Mittelbach, 1979). The forces behind the price surge are familiar. The costs of house production, land acquisition, and financing rose sharply. Increasingly stringent building codes and environmental regulations added to the burden. Inflationary expectations of the home-buying public and local growth controls contributed to price escalation. All of these hurt not only the poor but all first-time home buyers. By and large these forces emanated from the supply side.

On the demand side, imbalances between household growth in the typical home-entry ages and growth of their incomes made home purchase at rising prices an unattainable goal for many. The point becomes clear when the purchasing power of each group is analyzed. Purchasing power, or the total income earned by all households, is obtained as the product of the number of households in each age class and their average annual income. Figure 4.2 shows the contribution of the various age brackets to the total 1970–1980 increase in purchasing power (ΔPP), measured in terms of changes in the number of households (ΔHH) and incomes received (ΔY) by each. Total real purchasing power (in 1980 dollars), the reservoir of personal income from which housing expenditures is drawn, grew by $371 billion. Of every total dollar increase, 37 cents accrued to the group headed by persons aged 25–34.

If these households fared so well materially, what explains the affordability crisis? The charted data hint at an answer. When the sources of the increased purchasing power are separated it becomes clear that sheer growth of numbers, not rising incomes, accounted for the entry-

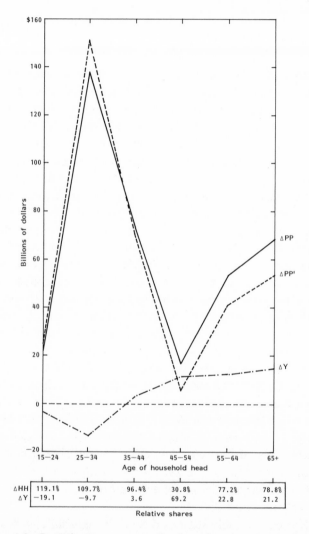

FIGURE 4.2. Contributions to growth of total consumer purchasing power (ΔPP) by changes in number of households (ΔHH) and per household income (ΔY), by age of householder, 1970–1980 (source: Table E.4).

age generation's entire gain. Mean real income per household in fact went from $21,843 in 1970 to $20,713 in 1980, down by 5.2%. If household incomes had remained unchanged, the group's purchasing power would have risen by $151 billion (the amounts assuming no change in real income per household are shown by the broken line in the chart and denoted $\Delta PP'$) instead of by $138 billion. Thus, while the number of households entering the home-buying age range burgeoned, their average income dropped. In housing terms, need rose but effective demand fell. Add to this the supply factors enumerated above and the roots of the trouble are exposed.

The analysis of the composition of the entry-group's purchasing power applies with nearly equal force to the next elder cohort, those headed by persons 35–44 years old. That group's contribution to the overall 1970–1980 increase in consumer purchasing power amounted to $74 billion, or one-fifth the total contributed by all households. As with their juniors, household growth was responsible for nearly all (95%) of the increase, with marginally higher incomes accounting for the remainder. Mean real household income rose from $25,825 in 1970 to $26,052 10 years later, a difference that could be attributed entirely to statistical error.

For the mature middle-aged, the sources of combined consumer purchasing power varied radically from those of the younger age groups. Rising real income per household contributed nearly 70% during the 1970s, while the increase of households was responsible for the rest of the purchasing power increment. Two factors explain the dominant role of income for the mature middle-aged. First, the number of these households is relatively small since the householders were born well before the onset of the postwar baby boom. Second, incomes at this life cycle stage have reached their lifetime peak and they are boosted by a higher proportion of multiple earners in the family.

Despite their comparatively low incomes, the economic status of the elderly has advanced remarkably. During the 1970s, their purchasing power grew by nearly $70 billion. While this was only half the increase registered by the home-entrant group, the income versus household components differed greatly. Real income growth per household contributed over one-fifth and household growth the remainder. In fact, the real gain in the aged's total purchasing power came to $15 billion, the largest amount for any age group. Even with the prospect of more moderate improvements in the future, elderly households constitute a group with vastly enlarged purchasing power that can at least in part be captured by the housing market.

DOES COHORT SIZE INFLUENCE INCOMES?

Is it mere coincidence that, in the recent past, incomes of fast-growing age cohorts—such as those 25–44—rose little or not at all, and those characterized by slow growth—for example, the 45–54 group—increased substantially? Easterlin's (1980) research linking the economic position of a generation with its size attempts to unravel the mechanism at work. According to his hypothesis, set out in Chapter 3 at greater length and in a broader context, a large generation, like the one resulting from the postwar baby boom, produces a large labor supply on entry into the work force, exceeding the demand for its services. Consequently, its wages and salaries are kept low and its unemployment runs high. The strong upward trend in the size of the entry group during the 1970s produced fierce competition for the available supply of jobs. Lowered earnings were the consequence. An empirical test of Easterlin's intriguing proposition confirms its validity.

The following test uses 1970 and 1980 data for numbers of households (rather than earners) arranged by life cycle stage[5] and household income (rather than earnings). Thus the test crudely approximates Easterlin's posited relationship. If the hypothesis holds, one would expect (1) income to be higher (lower) when cohorts are smaller (larger) and (2) income to decline (rise) with increasing (decreasing) cohort size. The data used for the tests are expressed in relatives rather than absolutes. Household income per age group (Y_a) is expressed as a ratio to average lifetime household income $(\bar{Y})$, and each age group of households (H_a) is expressed as a percent of the total number of households (H).[6] In keeping with Easterlin's claim, negative relationships are expected between both (1) $Y_a/\bar{Y}$ and H_a/H and (2) $\Delta Y_a/\bar{Y}$ and $\Delta H_a/H$.

According to the hypothesis, 1980 real income should exceed the 1970 level when household proportions are larger in the latter year, and income should be higher in 1970 than in 1980 when household proportions are smaller in 1980 than in 1970—all for corresponding age groups. The results of the test show that this is indeed the case (Figure 4.3).

The postwar baby boom appears in 1980 for households in the 15–24 age group and, even more dramati-

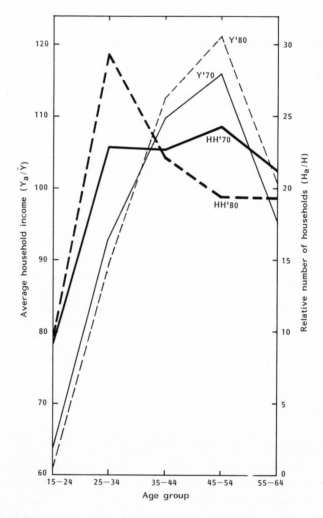

FIGURE 4.3. Relative number of households (H_a/H) and average household income ($Y_a/\bar{Y}$), by life cycle stage, 1970 and 1980 (source: Table E.3).

cally, in the 25–34 group, as each increased its proportions over the same age groups 10 years earlier. As expected, relative incomes were lower in 1980 than in 1970 for both cohorts. Households in the remaining three groups accounted for lower proportions of total households in 1980 than in 1970 and their relative incomes were higher, as the theory predicts, in 1980. The inverse relationship emerges with particular clarity in Figure 4.4, showing 1970–1980 percentage changes. For all age groups, the changes are in the expected direction and lend support to Easterlin's hypothesis.

In the future, the importance of the two key determinants of cohort size and income level will probably be

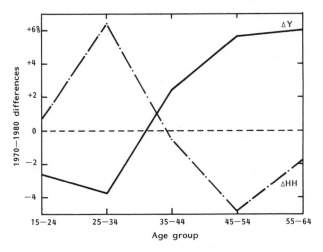

FIGURE 4.4. Relative number of households and average household income, by life cycle stage, 1970–1980 changes (source: Table E.3).

reversed. With additions to the labor force declining because the new generation of young adults is smaller, its per household real income is likely to grow faster than during the previous decade. Arrival of the postwar baby boom group at mature middle age during the latter 1980s and the 1990s will serve to blunt the earnings peak characterizing that life cycle stage.

Future shifts in the age and income distributions of the adult population are also likely to affect savings, the financial wherewithal of housing. During the remainder of the 1980s and into the 1990s, a record number of Americans will reach the 45–54 age bracket, a period when they begin to save; the number of adults moving into the 55–64 bracket when savings rates are at their peak, however, declines sharply. Whether the increased savings volume of the rapidly growing 45–54 group will be sufficient to offset the reduced savings of the shrinking 55–64 class is unpredictable. But the number of people entering young adulthood—typically net borrowers rather than net savers—will decline sharply. Hence, the demand for mortgage and other consumer credit by this group should be lower than in the recent past. While the availability and cost of funds for housing depends on a host of nondemographic variables, it appears that they will not be adversely affected by changes in the size of age cohorts alone.

APPENDIX E: DETAILED DATA ON SOCIOECONOMIC CHARACTERISTICS OF HOUSEHOLDS BY AGE OF HOUSEHOLD HEAD

TABLE E.1. Families with Own Children under 18 Living in Their Household, Percent Distribution by Age of Household Head, March 1984[a]

Age of household head	Percent of all families with Children[b]			Children per family
	Under 12	12–17	Total	
Under 25	8.4	0.1	6.1	1.45
25–34	48.4	5.8	36.8	1.89
35–44	34.8	44.7	37.5	2.03
45–54	7.1	36.7	15.2	1.61
55–64	1.1	11.3	3.9	1.36
65 and over	0.2	1.4	0.5	1.35
Total	100.0	100.0	100.0	1.85

[a]Source: U.S. Bureau of the Census (1985).
[b]Families include married couples and "single-spouse" families; average per family with children.

TABLE E.2. Mobility Ratios of Married Couples,
by Life Stage, Selected Years, 1973–1983[a,b]

Age	1973	1975	1977	1979	1981	1983
			Owners			
Under 35	35.9	29.0	37.3	30.9	32.2	20.5
35–44	11.3	10.1	14.0	12.0	7.5	6.6
45–64	5.6	4.8	6.4	5.7	3.4	3.5
65 and over	3.9	2.4	3.4	3.2	1.8	1.6
All ages	12.2	10.2	13.5	11.6	7.4	7.0
			Renters			
Under 35	103.1	119.7	104.0	98.4	98.0	76.4
35–44	46.4	47.0	52.6	49.5	53.1	44.9
45–64	27.0	29.0	31.5	28.8	28.2	26.7
65 and over	15.5	13.4	16.6	14.7	14.3	10.0
All ages	60.8	65.0	64.1	59.6	61.0	50.3

[a]Source: U.S. Bureau of the Census, *Annual Housing Survey*, Part D (various years).
[b]Mobility ratios are calculated as the number of recent movers, times 100, divided by the number of nonmovers. For households other than married couples, the age classification is less detailed (under 45, 45–64, and 65 and over), but the data show the same tendency for mobility to decline with increasing age.

TABLE E.3. Number of Households and Average Household
Incomes, Current and Constant (1980) Dollars,
by Life Stage, 1970 and 1980[a]

| Age of head | Households | | | | | |
| | 1970 | | 1980 | | Change 1970–1980 | |
	Number	%	Number	%	Number	%
14/15–24	4,707	7.3	6,443	7.8	1,736	36.9
25–34	11,847	18.4	19,153	23.3	7,306	61.7
35–44	11,739	18.2	14,462	17.6	2,723	23.2
45–54	12,509	19.4	12,694	15.4	185	1.5
55–64	10,952	17.0	12,704	15.4	1,752	16.0
65 +	12,622	19.7	16,912	20.5	4,290	34.0
All	64,376	100.0	82,368	100.0	17,992	28.0

| | Mean income per household | | | | | |
| | Current $ | | Constant (1980) $ | | | |
	1970	1980	1970	1980	Change	%Change
14/15–24	$ 7,115	$14,227	$15,070	$14,227	– $ 843	– 5.59
25–34	10,313	20,713	21,843	20,713	– 1130	– 5.17
35–44	12,193	26,052	25,825	26,052	227	+ 0.88
45–54	12,858	28,169	27,233	28,169	936	+ 3.44
55–64	10,573	23,504	22,394	23,504	1110	+ 4.96
65 +	5,418	12,628	11,475	12,628	1153	+ 10.05
All	10,001	21,063	21,182	21,063	– 119	– 0.56

[a]Sources: For 1970, U.S. Bureau of the Census, *Money Income of Households, Families, and Persons in the United States* (1971), Table 2; for 1980, U.S. Bureau of the Census, *Money Income of Households, Families, and Persons in the United States* (1982), Table 11.

TABLE E.4. Contributions to Growth of Total Consumer
Purchasing Power (ΔPP) by Changes in Number
of Households (ΔHH) and per Household Real Incomes (ΔY),
by Life Stage, 1970–1980 (Amounts in Millions of 1980 Dollars)[a]

Age of household head	ΔPP	$ Contribution to ΔPP[b]		% Contribution to ΔPP		% Distr. of ΔPP
		ΔHH	ΔY	ΔHH	ΔY	
15–24	$20,730	$24,698	– $3,968	119.1%	– 19.1%	5.6%
25–34	137,942	151,329	– 13,387	109.7	– 9.7	37.1
35–44	73,604	70,940	2,664	96.4	3.6	19.8
45–54	16,920	5,211	11,708	30.8	69.2	4.6
55–64	53,336	41,179	12,157	77.2	22.8	14.4
65 +	68,727	54,174	14,553	78.8	21.2	18.5
Total	$371,347	$379,008	– $7,661	102.1	– 2.1	100.0%

[a]Source: Same as Table E.3.
[b]Contributions to ΔPP are calculated as follows:
For the ΔHH share: $Y_{80}(HH_{80} - HH_{70})$
For the ΔY share: $HH_{70}(Y_{80} - Y_{70})$
Their sum equals ΔPP_{70-80}.

NOTES

1. The classification of the youngest group here differs from the 18–34 age bracket used in the statistical analysis in Chapter 2. The present chapter focuses on typology, and for this purpose it seems best to maintain 10-year intervals except for the open-end bracket of 65 years and over.

2. The *Annual Housing Surveys* from which these data are derived provide only limited age classifications for households other than married couples.

3. *Annual Housing Surveys*, U.S. Bureau of the Census (1973 through 1983). The mobility ratios exclude moves from housing units to institutional care facilities for the elderly.

4. However, the proportion of the elderly owning mobile homes in 1980, at 23.7% of all owner-occupied mobile homes, exceeded only moderately the proportion of the group in total households, at 20.4% (U.S. Bureau of the Census, *Annual Housing Survey*, 1980, Part A). No comparable data are available for condominiums.

5. Because the hypothesis relates earnings to cohort size, and the active labor force is usually confined to persons under age 65, the 65 + cohort is omitted from the analysis. The lowest age category was 15–24 years in 1980 and 14–24 in 1970. The analysis was repeated omitting this cohort and produced the same results.

6. In symbols, the hypotheses are

$Y_a/\bar{Y} = f(H_a/H)$ (1)

$\Delta Y_a/\bar{Y} = f(\Delta H_a/H)$ (2)

where Δs measure first differences.

REFERENCES

Avery, R. T., Elliehausen, G. E., and Canner, G. B. (1984). Survey of consumer finances. *Federal Reserve Bulletin, 70*(9), 679–692.

Easterlin, R. A. (1980). *Birth and Fortune: The impact of numbers on personal welfare.* New York: Basic Books.

Feldstein, M. (1985). The social security explosion. *Public Interest,* No. 81, 94–106.

Fuchs, V. R. (1983). *How we live.* Cambridge, MA: Harvard University Press.

Fuchs, V. R. (1984). Though much is taken—Reflections on aging, health, and medical care. *Milbank Memorial Fund Quarterly: Health and Society, 62*(2).

Glick, P. (1957). *American families.* New York: Wiley.

Grebler, L. and Mittelbach, F. G. (1979). *The inflation of house prices.* Lexington, MA: Lexington Books.

Guttentag, J. M. (1975). Creating new financial instruments for the aged. In *Bulletin of the Center for the Study of Financial Institutions.* New York: New York University.

Longman, P. (1985). Justice between generations. *Atlantic Monthly, 255*(6), 73–81.

Michael, T., Fuchs, V. R., and Scott, S. R. (1980). Changes in the propensity to live alone: 1950–1976. *Demography, 17*(1), 38–56.

Mitchell, O. S., and Fields, G. S. (1984). The economics of retirement behavior. *Journal of Labor Economics, 2*(1), 84–105.

Rosen, K., and Smith, L. (1982). The ''used house'' market. Berkeley, CA: Center for Real Estate and Urban Land Studies, University of California.

Scholen, K. and Chen, Y.-P. (Eds.). (1980). *Unlocking home equity for the elderly.* Cambridge, MA: Ballinger.

Shanas, E. (1980). Older people and their families, the new pioneers. *Journal of Marriage and the Family, 42*(1).

Troll, L. E. (1971). The family of later life: A decade review. *Journal of Marriage and the Family, 33,* 263–290.

U.S. Bureau of the Census. (various years). *Annual Housing Survey.* Washington, D.C.: U.S. Government Printing Office.

U.S. Bureau of the Census. (various years). *Current population reports,* Series P-20. Washington, D.C.: U.S. Government Printing Office.

U.S. Bureau of the Census. (1971). *Income in 1970 of families and persons in the*

United States. Current Population Reports, Series P-60, No. 80. Washington, D.C.: U.S. Government Printing Office.

U.S. Bureau of the Census. (1982). *Money income of households, families, and persons in the United States: 1980.* Current Population Reports, Series P-60. No. 132. Washington, D.C.: U.S. Government Printing Office.

U.S. Bureau of the Census. (1983). *Current Population Reports, An aging society,* Special Studies, Series P-23, No. 128. Washington, D.C.: U.S. Government Printing Office.

U.S. Bureau of the Census. (1985). *Current population reports, household and family characteristics,* Series P-20, No. 398. Washington, D.C.: U.S. Government Printing Office.

U.S. Bureau of Labor Statistics. (1982). *Economic projections to 1990,* Bulletin 2121. Washington, D.C.: U.S. Government Printing Office.

5

The Housing of the Future
DEMAND CHANGES AND SUPPLY RESPONSE

Demographic forces already under way and accelerating through the rest of this century will tend to weaken housing demand, though at a moderate degree. That prognosis, based on the analysis of previous chapters, raises a crucial question. Can one foresee countervailing forces that will offset or reduce the negative influence of demographic conditions?

It is the thrust of this chapter to develop an affirmative answer. We believe that improvements in housing *quality* together with additional services rendered by dwellings have the potential for canceling or at least moderating the effects of adverse population trends, and we shall support this thesis at some length. We shall show that potent factors on the demand side will operate in favor of quality improvements and that suppliers can be expected to respond to them in a positive way.

In doing so, we concentrate on the outlook for new residential investment rather than the number of newly built housing units, the conventional measure used in projections.

There are good reasons for this shift in focus. Residential investment includes not only new construction but also capital spending on the alteration and modernization of existing dwellings, and this component is likely to increase substantially in absolute volume as well as relative to new building. Further, dollar calculations determine the incentives for housing producers and their suppliers to expand or contract their output. The entrepreneurial "bottom line," net profit, is also expressed in dollars. So are the house prices or rents paid by consumers. At the macro level of national income accounts, it is residential investment, not the number of dwelling units built, that reveals the position of housing in total real output and in aggregate fixed investment.

As for capital spending on the upgrading of existing structures, this component of residential investment is of considerable magnitude. The reported "additions and alterations," the statistical equivalent of such spending, amounted to $1 for every $4 of new housing construction expenditures during the 1960–1983 period—and it is probably an understatement since a good bit of this work is done without building permits, which form the basis for the official estimates. Further upgrading of the housing stock may benefit, among other things, from gentrification, the movement of young middle-class households into rundown neighborhoods which they proceed to rehabilitate.

The anticipated shift to higher-quality housing contradicts the widespread current opinion that the future belongs to the stripped-down single-family or apartment building, with a minimum of frills and equipment. This view is derived from the recent "affordability" crisis. One must be on guard, however, against projecting short- or intermediate-term conditions into the long-run future. The affordability crisis was unique to an era when households mushroomed in number but real incomes failed to rise for those seeking to realize the American dream of homeownership. But this disjunction is, happily, a passing phenomenon if future trends bear out projections. Figure 5.1 shows the relative contributions of changes in household numbers to purchasing power for future years, as well as for the critical 1970s.

As the data confirm, household growth alone accounted for all of the increase in purchasing power during the past decade. If the forward estimates in Figure 5.1 materialize—and they are quite reasonable—the picture will be vastly different in the future.[1] The relative importance of household growth will decline and that of real income growth will increase. In fact, whereas income's contribution in the 1970s was nil, by the early 1990s it is projected to account for over 60% of purchasing power growth. (The dashed line in the graph, denoted $\Delta PP'$, shows the purchasing power amounts in the absence of real income changes.) Thus, while the need for new dwellings to accommodate young, newly formed households declines, the capability of households to demand housing rises and, very likely, the amount invested per dwelling unit will increase accordingly.

This is not to deny that dwelling units *may* on average get smaller. The compact townhouse may become increasingly popular and displace the free-standing home with its larger yard space and lot size. But these changes,

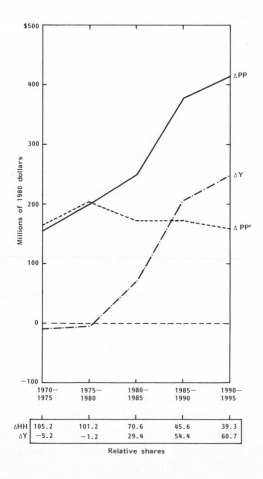

FIGURE 5.1. Contributions to growth of total consumer purchasing power (ΔPP) by changes in number of households (ΔHH) and per household income (ΔY), by 5-year intervals, 1970–1995 (source: Table F.1).

if continued, would merely help to resolve the historical paradox of ever smaller households versus dwelling units of more or less constant size in the housing stock, a discrepancy that has given rise to the charge of growing underutilization of our residential real estate resources (Baer, 1979; Gellen, 1983, 1984). In this context, it is well to keep in mind that, barring major disaster, most of the dwelling units constituting the stock at the turn of the next century have already been built. Nevertheless, conversion of the existing housing stock offers opportunities for replacing large with smaller units, as it has done in the past.

More important, a decline in the average size of units is entirely compatible with greater quality and larger real investment per unit. If quality improvements are substantial, total residential investment can expand in the long run even if the average size of units decreases. We shall return to the issue of dwelling-unit size at a later stage of analysis.

QUANTITY VERSUS QUALITY—
THE PERENNIAL ALTERNATIVES

It is no novelty to say that housing is bought or rented for the services it provides. The duration and scope of these services, but also the way they are utilized gives housing its utility and value. The services are of many kinds: shelter; privacy; accessibility to the workplace, schools, shopping, and other facilities; desirability of the neighborhood; and even the prestige of a good address. When consumers make housing decisions under the constraint of their capacity to pay, they are typically trading off these against other attributes of housing services. One of the most frequent and most important trade-offs is the one between the quantity and quality of housing.

Thus, at a maximum outlay determined by its circumstances, a household may choose a centrally air-conditioned residence with a smaller living room instead of one with a larger living room but lacking the comfort of air-conditioning. At lower income levels, consumers may decide in favor of a unit with a kitchen large enough for family meals or ancillary activities such as children's schoolwork and compromise on the number of bathrooms.

Technology has facilitated the trade-off. Compare the space required for the wood-burning stove in common use during the 19th century with today's compact range top with space underneath or above for storage or ovens. Similar technological changes can be expected in the future. Another kind of trade-off occurs when homeowners decide to purchase an old and obsolete property at a low enough price to enable them to make the additional investment for upgrading its quality within their financial capacity. On the supply side, builders planning single-family or apartment houses in a given location and price range have always engaged in trade-offs between the size of dwellings and their quality in terms of exterior and interior materials, workmanship, and the number and reputation of equipment and fixtures provided. They are in effect betting on consumer acceptance of products incorporating the builders' judgment about the relative importance of quantitative and qualitative attributes of residential properties.

The recent literature on hedonic prices, using multivariate analysis that imputes prices to the various physical components of dwelling units, has contributed greatly to an understanding of trade-offs.[2] A detailed study based on this method, for example, has measured the relative importance of housing quantity, quality, and location for rental units, and it is of special interest because the data apply to decisions of moderate-income households eligible for participation in HUD's housing allowance experiment. Even for this group, most of the increased residential consumption made possible by federal allowance payments was brought about by better quality rather than more space; further, the relative significance of quality components rose with higher income. Expenditures for improved location showed an irregular relationship to income (Barnett, 1979; especially pp. 42–47).

A single study confined to one area or period of time cannot be definitive. In conjunction with the widespread observation of trade-offs between housing quantity and quality, however, it supports the notion that such trade-offs have always been an important part of consumer decisions. Hence, it is only a small step to argue that future decisions will favor quality over space, particularly under conditions of rising real income. The next section discusses the reasons for this projection.

THE CASE FOR QUALITY IMPROVEMENTS

In other times and places, the most valuable inheritance was the ancestral home. But, in the Untied States, who wants to live in his father's—much less his grandfather's—house? Upward-mobile Americans might not even want to live in that neighborhood! [Daniel J. Boorstin. (1976). *The Exploring Spirit: America and the World, Then and Now*].

Put briefly, the anticipated demand for housing of better quality comes from two sources: (1) the need for time-saving devices to facilitate household operations, greatly reinforced by the growth of the female labor force and increasing opportunity cost of household labor, and (2) the prospective transfer to the dwelling place of activities and functions previously performed outside the home. Both rest largely but not wholly on technological progress, the trademark of the 20th century. Both extend trends already under way. Each requires elaboration.

Mechanization of Household Operations

The installation of equipment to facilitate household chores has a venerable history: the vacuum cleaner, central heating and cooling, the refrigerator, washing machine, and dishwasher, the improved oven, the all-electric kitchen, the home freezer, and, more recently, the microwave oven are the most notable examples. Whether these and other devices are furnished by the builder or bought by the consumer makes no difference for our analysis. Other means of simplifying household operations reflect technology developed outside the home. Cases in point are precooked frozen or take-out foods to ease meal preparation, more powerful detergents for cleaning, and clothing made from synthetic fibers.

Paralleling these innovations has been the decline of domestic servants, a cause and at the same time an effect of household mechanization. The number of ''private household workers'' dropped from 1.54 million in 1950 to less than a million in 1984, continuing an earlier trend. (U.S. Bureau of the Census, 1975, 1985a) Even more impressive, there were 3.2 domestic helpers per 1000 households in 1950 but less than 1.2 in 1984. Their displacement has been partly offset by a commercial innovation: the emergence of housecleaning contractors whose services can be hired for a day, week, or month, or any other time interval.

Devices already in existence or yet to be developed will further intensify household mechanization. Electronically timed switches can regulate heating and cooling, turn on and off lights and appliances, and water the garden—all on predetermined timetables that obviate the need for householders to remember chores or be at home. Electronic parts grafted on telephones make phoning easier. The home computer will replace the rather primitve ways in which most consumers keep their financial accounts and family budgets, handle the replacement of food and other inventories, and arrange timely payments to suppliers of goods and services and even to the tax collector. Besides, the home computer is already adding to the ''fun and games'' available for family entertainment. Video recorders allow TV programs to be stored and seen at times suiting the viewers convenience. Intercom systems facilitate communication among household members instead of the present ''methods'' of running stairs or corridors or shouting from one room to the other. Automated burglar alarms, smoke detectors, and life-saving devices enhance the protective functions of the home.

Clearly, microtechnologies can have important impacts on household operation. As an extreme example, a newspaper account (Pennisi, 1985, p. VIII-26) describes

a "totally computerized" home equipped with 13 computers, 14 telephones, 26 TV monitors, 8 miles of wiring, and a battery of video cameras and video cassette
recorders, and robots substituting for pets. In the newly
completed showcase, dubbed by its owners FutureHome
and located in Texas (where else?), technology relays
information to the occupants via telephone to notify
them whether the temparature in the hot tub is warm
enough, whether the children have arrived home from
school, whether the pantry (under video surveillance) is
stocked with ingredients needed for tonight's dinner,
and whether the person in the den is a welcome guest
or an intruder. And, perhaps most important of all, a
computer makes and answers phone calls.

The typical price reductions of novel technical equipment as production volume increases will spread its use
from the rich to the well-to-do and then to the broad
middle class.[3] Besides, the demographic analysis in
earlier sections has indicated that the number of households headed by middle-aged people will grow substantially in the coming years. These households are typically
at or near the peak of their lifetime earnings. Part of their
income is available for discretionary spending, and it is
reasonable to expect that improved housing quality will
be one of the favored objects of such spending. Many
of the middle-aged have also accumulated financial assets that can be converted into durable household assets.
If the objective of better-quality housing cannot be met
by moving into a modern dwelling, consumers will upgrade their existing accommodations and purchase the
equipment made available by innovation, as demonstrated by the incipient growth of home computers.

Even the aged are likely target-markets for upgrading their homes with new technologies. Given their rapidly increased purchasing power, they will demand more in-home amenities like sunrooms, small hot-water tubs, and saunas that ease medical problems such as arthritis. The more affluent retired persons who tend to stroll regularly for health maintenance and to travel more than those confined to a regular work schedule will demand security devices that protect their home and person while they are en route.

New Functions of the Dwelling Place

Defined broadly, housing quality includes the variety of activities that can be performed in the dwelling place. Variety is already on the increase even without the benefit of new technology. The "granny flat" attached to the family home is just one of numerous examples. It seems that the widespread preference for the nuclear family is being modified in favor of a limited form of the extended family of bygone days—and in a way that combines proximity with privacy. There has been a rediscovery of grandparents' usefulness in a family household with children where both parents are working outside the home. Whether the granny flat is indeed occupied by a close relative is an immaterial detail. Another case is the increasing use of the dwelling place for professional purposes, often involving less than strict compliance with zoning ordinances. The psychologist or the economist consultant, for example, may have his or her office in the previous formal dining room and convert the former children's room into storage space for files. Small business is also increasingly conducted from the home. The carpentry contractor or the couple engaged in direct merchandising or the woman doing consumer survey work over the phone are cases in point. These practices are bound to grow as professional services expand and technology makes workplaces more ubiquitous.

The internalization of services in the home is already pronounced for some activities such as entertainment and recreation. Television provided without cost and now by cable at moderate cost has diminished the urge for going to the movies. Videotapes of movies can be rented for home shows at less than half the price of a single admission or at a fraction of what it costs to take the whole family out to the cinema. The exercise machine and other home gym equipment replace the walk to the park or the trip to a health club. A martini at home in the Jacuzzi replaces the drink after work with the boys.

The potentials for home entertainment will be greatly enhanced when the present one-way telecommunication technology is augmented by two-way capability, already achieved technically but not yet ready for household use. Among the possibilities are "live" audience responses, participation in quiz shows, interactive instruction, shopping, ticket purchases, and consumer or political polls, to name a few.

Even buying habits are at the point of change. The volume of direct merchandise offerings from catalogs distributed not only by mail-order firms but by oil companies and other nonretailers has increased by leaps and bounds, thanks largely to the invention of the credit card and the low-cost exchange of lists of card-holders. Consumers can now select a broad range of goods in the privacy of their homes and save the time and energy spent in shops. This change is apt to accelerate not only because of its convenience but also because the sales personnel in so many stores are no longer capable of advising customers on the quality of merchandise. The difference between selecting goods from store displays or from a catalog has narrowed.

Shopping for knowledge and information, as well as for goods, can be internalized into the home through existing technology. In Europe, cable connections and teletext already provide instant access to a broad selection of information ranging from weather reports to encyclopedia extracts, all at the touch of a button. The U.S. counterpart, the electronic bulletin board, has recently made its debut, heralded as the most revolutionary breakthrough in information delivery since the telegraph and telephone replaced the Pony Express over a century ago. Until recently the preserve of young computer bugs, electronic bulletin boards are increasingly used as a communications medium by a broader spectrum of the population because they are cheaper, more accessible, and less regulated than any other national medium. The devices dispense legal advice, stock market tips, airline schedules, and even electronic prayers.

These and similar innovations are not space-age fantasy. Take the case of electronic mail, a development akin to electronic bulletin boards. Revenues of $200 million in 1984 classified the producers as members of a fledgling industry, yet electronic mail usage is booming ahead at an annual growth rate of nearly 60%—the fastest of any segment of the computer industry. Today an estimated 1 million consumers have electronic "mailboxes" (Rempel, 1985, p. VI-1). Aside from their commercial applications, the new information technologies compress activity into the home, giving householders instant, easy, and cheap access to information without having to go outdoors, not even to the postal mailbox.

Technology serves not only consumption but production as well, for "futurists" foresee an even greater evolution of the dwelling place through innovations which allow the wholesale transfer to the home of work functions now performed elsewhere. A case in point is the displacement of work from offices or even from factories. Efficiency is invoked as the driving force for this development, and the elimination of the journey to and from work illustrates only the most obvious efficiency gains (Nilles, 1976). Technology plays a key role in the transfer of work functions to the home. Alvin Toffler, the most persistent prophet of societal change induced by technology, anticipates a ''low cost work-station in any home, providing it with a 'smart' typewriter along with a facsimile machine or computer console and teleconferencing equipment'' (Toffler, 1980, p. 197).

''Telecommuting'' will offer many advantages to those who can move their work to themselves rather than moving themselves to the workplace. Apart from the obvious economies in commuting time and cost that accrue to telecommuters (and the reduced traffic congestion that benefits the urban public at large), working at atypical times and places provides flexibility. Telecommuters can follow their own schedule, working at hours when others are sleeping or engaged in other nonwork activities. They have more time to spend with their families or to get work done undisturbed by normal office routines.

Toffler's prophecy of ''electronic cottages'' dotting the townscape may be overdrawn. Wholesale work transfers to the dwelling will meet obstacles from many directions. Employers may resist it for fear that they would lose control over performance (unless piece rates were substituted for hourly wages or weekly salaries) or that coordination would become a far more difficult task. Employees may reject it because of isolation in the home and the loss of human interaction offered in the workplace. Labor unions may be opposed since it is hard to organize workers spread over numerous residences rather than physically concentrated in large establishments.

Yet, the potentials of modern technology for redistributing jobs between workplace and dwelling place cannot be denied. Older technology has done so in the past. Housing in the preindustrial era often served as a locus of production as well as consumption, notably in textile manufacture. It was only with the industrial revolution and the requirement that production be a group effort focused on an assembly line that workplace and residence became increasingly separated. The ongoing technical revolution promises to have the opposite effect in some and perhaps in many occupations. If the promises hold, the dwelling place will increase in utility and, with it, value. Before long, this transformation will call not only for redesign of residential buildings but also for revisions of zoning ordinances and city planning principles, both of which have been dominated by the notion of strict separation of residential and nonresidential land use.

While many new functions will be performed in the house of tomorrow, others, notably the raising of children, will diminish in importance. Child rearing will take less time among household activities, continuing a long trend. We have already noted the role of child-care centers as an alternative to mother's care in the home. The number of children per household has also diminished steadily; a woman born in the 1950s typically bore fewer than half as many children—1.5 against 3.2— as did her counterpart born 20 years earlier (Glick, 1977).

But even more remarkable is the relatively short period encompassed by a family's child-rearing obligations today compared to yesteryear. A woman born in the 1950s has devoted an average of 20 years of her life to raising her children, a substantial drop from the length of time so spent by her elders. Women born prior to World War II, for example, typically spent at least 25 years rearing children (Figure 5.2). That change is explained simply by the decline in the number of children the average woman bears and the shorter interval between the birth of the first and last. For example, for a woman born in the 1880s, 9 years elapsed between her first and last child's birth; the average woman born in the 1950s had all of her children within a period of only 2.6 years.

When the life cycle data are related to the number of years of married life an average couple spends together it becomes clear that a vastly increasing proportion of a family lifetime is spent without children at home. A woman marrying at the turn of the century could count on 80% of her family years with kids in residence. In contrast, her modern contemporary can count on spending over half of her married life with her spouse but without children at home. Most of the change can be attributed to greater longevity plus fewer years elapsing between the first birth and departure of the lastborn from the nest. Yet most of the standing stock of housing was built to accommodate child rearing. In the "old days," space in the home built and equipped for raising children was used almost continuously for that purpose; today that space is used less than half the time for its intended purpose.

Root Cause: The Economics of Time

The adage "time is money" has been heeded again and again in the development of modern production

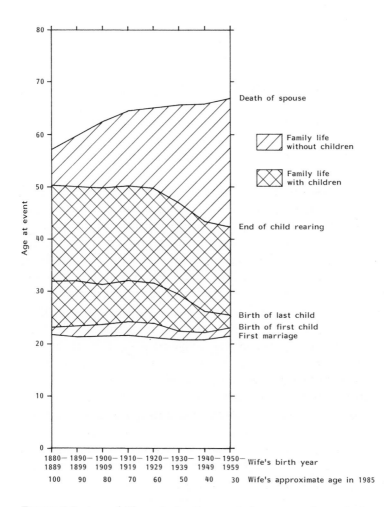

FIGURE 5.2. Age of life cycle family events for women born during the 1880s to 1950s (source: Adapted from Glick, 1977).

techniques but has received little attention in the study of consumer behavior. Among the notable exceptions is Staffan B. Linder's work (1970) on the economics of time. Linder demonstrates convincingly that the value of time spent on nonwork (consumption) increases as the value of work time rises with economic growth, yielding higher real income. To restore equilibrium, consumers seek to enhance the return on consumption time as the yield on work time improves. They do so by increasing the amount of consumer goods and services enjoyed per unit of time.

This reasoning is directly applicable to household operations which absorb a large proportion of the time devoted to consumption. Indeed, people on average spend more time at home than at any other place. According to a time-budget study for 44 U.S. cities, an astonishing three-quarters of the urban population's time is spent at home; the corresponding figure for urban adults is 68%, with time at work absorbing only 20% (Szalai, 1966). With rising real income, the opportunity cost of time spent on the consumption of housing services also rises. Just as manufacturers replace labor with machines when wage costs mount, householders substitute equipment for manual work when consumption time becomes more valuable. The practical consequences of this principle have greatly gained in importance since more and more women are foresaking their traditional role as unpaid guardians of the home for paid jobs outside the home. While real wages have multiplied in the long run, there has been no corresponding increase in the rewards of domestic work.

Another important factor favoring the purchase of time-economizing devices for the home, also a consequence of increasing time value, is the maturing of the baby boom generation into middle age when both lifetime earnings and the opportunity costs of time reach their peak. Under these conditions, the mechanization of household operations is far more compelling than it used to be. Since the dramatic growth of women in the labor force is of such recent origin, technological progress in the home remains in an early stage and is bound to intensify. Home technology will become a major growth industry.

A lively debate has emerged over the question whether the past mechanization of household chores has reduced the time of doing them, mainly the housewife's time (Markusen, 1983; Scott, 1982; Robinson, 1980; Vanek, 1978). The statistical findings are not impressive but they are also mostly inconclusive or flawed by inadequate procedures. In any event, they are of no predictive value with respect to home technology yet to be developed. Among other things, they fail to take proper account of the "polychronic" use of time that is facilitated by modern devices, that is, the doubling up (or tripling up) of activities performed at the same time, enhancing the utility of time expenditures. When a unit of time is absorbed by a single activity, time is used monochronically. Eating in silence, and *only* eating, is a commonplace example. When several tasks can be performed in a unit of time, the latter is used polychronically. Thus, the time taken for meals can also be spent on discussion of the day's activities with other household members, or on conversation about current world affairs, or on reading the paper or watching the news telecast.

Many existing home gadgets already allow the polychronic use of time. In the presence of modern technology (and a reasonably well-designed housing unit), the housewife can simultaneously cook the evening meal, watch Julia Child on television for pointers or listen to the hi-fi turned on in the background, perhaps, with the aid of closed-circuit TV, mind the children playing upstairs, and all the while have yesterday's laundry churning in the washing machine. If the meal is prepared in a timed and programmed microwave oven, time is freed to play with the kids or help them with schoolwork or do the bills while dinner cooks. The husband can use his woodwork equipment to indulge in his hobby and at the same time entertain the children by showing his know-how and assigning them some easy tasks.

We project that suppliers will respond to the increasing value of consumption time by continuing to develop household innovations that save time and foster its polychronic use. Because of the prospective growth of middle-aged households with relatively high discretionary spending power, the supply response will probably focus on this group.

Much of what is offered in the mail-order catalogs that daily fill our mailboxes is gimmickry, but some devices that even an H. G. Wells could not have imagined a short decade ago serve more useful functions. Already, a clothes dryer being marketed now senses the amount of moisture in the load and automatically shuts off the machine when clothes are dry. A range that allows cooking by gas and microwave simultaneously within a single oven makes it possible to brown foods yet cook them quickly. Refrigerators are available with sensors warning when the temperature inside creeps beyond predetermined limits. Computers can read cooking instructions from a bar code on a frozen food package and automatically set the defrosting and cooking times on a microwave oven. Semiconductors that control the speed and power of appliance motors can dramatically cut energy consumption. Appliances of the future, equipped with voice synthesis and speech recognition devices, can respond to verbal commands, a boon to the elderly and handicapped.

Apart from conserving increasingly precious time and making routine jobs more attractive, the technology of tomorrow's home offers the promise of luring husbands and older children into the kitchen and laundry. Attracted by the dazzle of digital displays and multilighted control panels, those who formerly scorned ''womens' work'' will be tempted to lend a hand with the household chores that mother used to do but can't do now that she has a job.

Main Effect: Increased Value of the Home

The growing mechanization of household operations and even moderate activity transfers from the workplace to the dwelling place will enhance the services rendered by the home or lead to their intensification. Additional space will be needed in many cases to accommodate new equipment. Hence, the utility of the residence as a place that internalizes previously external activities is apt to increase and, since utility confers value, so does its worth.

These novel though elementary points lend potent support to the thesis that per-unit residential investment, including real expenditures for new construction and alteration and modernization plus household equipment, will rise in the future. In all probability, the technological innovations will also raise average investment per unit throughout the housing stock and therefore the total value of the stock.[4] This trend will counteract or may even overcome the negative influence on residential investment resulting from the demographically induced slowdown in the rate of additions to the housing inventory measured in terms of dwelling units.

In this projected framework, the issue of the future average size of housing units loses much of its significance. The mechanization of the household also makes it more difficult to predict change because unit size will be subject to cross-currents. Some of the innovations do not require more space. For example, the personal computer can be installed on a desk in the den or in the little second-floor space under the attic staircase that once served as a sewing room; the microwave oven can often be placed in the kitchen without enlarging its space. Some new functions in the home, such as professional services, can be accommodated by converting existing rooms or by arrangements for their more efficient multiple use. Others, like Toffler's electronic workshop, will in most cases add to space needs.

The present and future gadgets that cater to the family's recreation may also require space. The screening room, once the luxury of movie moguls, may become as common as the two-car garage. Further, dwelling space will expand to accommodate new nontechnological uses: granny flats, in-laws apartments, companion units to serve elderly occupants, or the "mingles" for two households who share kitchen and other common facilities (Gellen, 1983, 1984). Whether attached to the home as a "wing" or detached as compact garden cottages or placed on an additional floor, these uses generally require more space if a modicum of privacy is to be preserved.

The "affordability crisis" and statistics showing recent declines in the average size of newly built dwelling units have led many forecasters to predict that tomorrow's house will be smaller and more compact than yesteryear's. The preceding analysis casts doubt on these predictions. The shadow of doubt is lengthened by the results of a recent survey of nearly 5000 households undertaken by the MIT–Harvard Joint Center, which showed that most wanted larger homes (MIT–Harvard Joint Center for Urban Studies, 1984, p. 2). The respondents' two major areas of dissatisfaction with their present accommodations were insufficient privacy afforded by yards or other outside space, and lack of interior space.

Nor do the statistics on the actual size of new single-family houses show a *trend* toward smaller units. True, they reveal a reduction from an average of 1740 square feet in 1980 to 1710 in 1982 and 1725 in 1983 (U.S. Bureau of the Census, 1985a). But the small decline occurred in a period of economic recession. In fact, no long-term trend is discernible in the data stretching back to the 1960s. Instead, average size fluctuated in rough correspondence with the business cycle.

On balance, new living arrangements and new technology that raises per capita space consumption may help modify the present underutilization of the housing stock. Most of the anticipated spatial changes are only feasible in the owner-occupied sector of the housing supply where households have a high degree of discretion over property use (subject to public regulation). For that matter, underutilization in that sector is more frequent than in the rental stock.[5]

STAGNATION OF HOMEOWNERSHIP

The homeownership rate has inched up barely 2.5 percentage points in two decades. The slow increase has continued in the early 1980s, with the 1983 Housing Survey showing 64.7%.[6] The sluggish growth suggests a new era of stagnation in homeownership, so often hailed as an essential part of the "American Dream."

If there is any single overwhelming determinant of homeownership, it is real income. In 1973–1983, the median income of owners averaged nearly $21,000 in 1980 dollars, as against only $11,500 for renters. However, owners' real income was barely sustained over time while that of renters was declining (Figure 5.3). In other words, the income trend did not provide a stimulus for expanding the ownership rate.

While public attention focused on the home-buying boom of the 1970s and the opportunities of hedging inflation by home purchase, the number of renters becoming homeowners was to a large extent offset by the reverse tenure shift. In the 1973–1981 period, 16 million households changed from renter to owner status but, surprisingly, another 11 million changed from ownership to tenancy—a reflection of the growing numbers of truncated families, singles, and the elderly, plus the rise in mortgage interest rates.[7] Also, the ownership and condominium market, stimulated by the inflationary expectations of the 1970s, drained rental housing of many of its more prosperous tenants. Approximately 360,000 apartments were lost by conversion to condominiums and cooperatives during the 1970s and, according to HUD estimates, another 1.1 million were expected to go

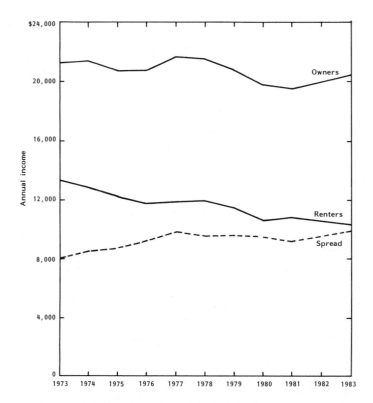

FIGURE 5.3. Median real income of homeowners and renters, 1973–1983 (1980 dollars); spread equals owners' less renters' incomes; data for 1982 interpolated (source: U.S. Bureau of the Census, *Annual Housing Survey*, various years).

the same route before 1986 (U.S. Department of Housing and Urban Development, 1980).

But this process cannot go on forever. Rental housing has more and more become a ''poor man's good'' and has been occupied increasingly by households other than married couples.[8] Since such households are poorer candidates for home purchase than the conjugal families, the reservoir of renters capable of acquiring ownership status has diminished. As shown in Table 5.1, single-spouse families and individuals, already a slight majority of all renters in 1973, represented nearly two-thirds in 1981. (Their share in total homeowners has also risen but has remained relatively small.) The median income position of single-spouse families and individuals who rent is greatly inferior to that of married couples in the same tenure class.[9] Their homeownership rate is well below 50% compared to about 75% for married couples.[10]

Hence, the growing concentration of households other than conjugal families in rental housing does not augur well for further progress of homeownership. The market for owner-occupied homes will continue to draw on the "cream of the crop" among renters, but that

TABLE 5.1. Household Composition and Median Household Income of Homeowners and Renters, 1973, 1977, and 1981[a]

Household type	Household composition			Median income (1980 $)		
	1973	1977	1981	1973	1977	1981
Owners	100.0%	100.0%	100.0%	$21,300	$21,714	$19,706
Married couples	75.5	74.4	72.0	24,078	25,107	23,141
Single-spouse	10.7	11.9	12.3	17,670	15,903	15,127
Individuals	13.8	13.7	15.7	7,409	7,871	8,045
Renters	100.0	100.0	100.0	13,336	11,943	10,576
Married couples	47.9	40.5	37.5	17,596	16,421	14,644
Single-spouse	20.8	25.1	27.3	12,156	9,260	8,239
Individuals	31.3	34.4	35.2	8,335	8,550	8,135

[a]Source: Bureau of the Census, *Annual Housing Survey* (various years).

group is getting smaller. This conclusion is reinforced by the estimated future growth of the various kinds of households. According to the projections in Chapter 2, the number of households other than married couples will increase by 23% in the 1985–1995 period compared to only 15% for husband-wife families, continuing the differential trends of the recent past.

The analysis confirms the strategic role that income plays as a determinant of tenure choice within the restraints imposed by the relative cost of owning and renting. Changes in the composition of households influence homeownership mainly through the income hierarchy descending from married couples to other families and single-person households. The homeownership rate is also correlated with age of household head, increasing with advancing age except for senior households. But age, in turn, is positively associated with income, as shown in Table F.2. Hence, there is a great deal of collinearity between age and income of owner-occupants.

In the future, the decline of young adults will diminish the potential reservoir of first-time home buyers. The shift to a larger proportion of middle-aged household heads will add to the number of owners but not augment the homeownership *rate* significantly since it is already high in this age group. The share in total households of single-spouse families and single-person households—units characterized by moderate ownership rates—will continue to increase, though at a slower pace than in the past.

Hence, projected demographic changes will not serve to promote homeownership materially. Only a major increase in real household income, a departure from the experience of the 1970s, would advance the homeownership rate over its current level of about two-thirds of all occupied housing units. Even so, the income tax revisions debated at this writing, whatever their general merits, cast a shadow on the prospects for homeownership. If enacted, they would raise the after-tax cost of ownership, although the extent would depend on which one of the proposals is adopted.

FUTURE TRENDS ON THE SUPPLY SIDE

The previous sections have already highlighted those long-run changes on the supply side of housing which we consider paramount. Suppliers will seek to adjust their product mix to meet the demand for higher-quality dwellings. The volume of modernization and alteration work in upgrading existing housing will expand relative to new construction. Hence, business will shift from firms that build homes or multifamily projects to contractors who are geared to the "messy" operations involved in quality improvements of the standing stock of residences. But builders and general contractors do not constitute entirely different industries. Depending on market conditions, many entrepreneurs in both groups have long since moved from new construction to the renovation of older buildings and vice versa.

These shifts are evident in statistics for the components of the total dollar value of private residential construction. The renovation market absorbs a growing portion of the industry's resources when the volume of new construction slackens; a return to more prosperous conditions signals a shift from the alterations and additions segment of the market back to new construction. In so doing, this type of resource mobility contributes a measure of overall stability to the residential building industry. For every dollar spent on alterations and additions during the 1960s and 1970s, $4.40 was spent for new housing units. In the 1980–1982 period, however, the sharp decline of new construction was accompanied by a more moderate drop in the volume of alterations and additions; the ratio of new construction spending to outlays for alterations and additions fell below $3 to $1. The recovery of building activity in 1983–1984 nearly restored the average ratio of previous decades (U.S. Department of Commerce, various).[11]

Because of intraindustry resource mobility, the projected greater opportunities in modernization and alteration work will not entail major adjustments by the construction industry. The only exception is the large merchant builder or apartment house sponsor who would find it difficult and certainly less efficient to organize his enterprise for the retail activity of upgrading dwellings on widely scattered sites. That activity thrives on low overhead costs and often requires technical on-the-spot decisions to cope with unforeseen conditions in existing structures. Thus, the anticipated growth of alteration and modernization favors small business.

In addition to the demographic factors already cited, another long-term force shifting construction toward alteration and renovation is the increasing importance that society is giving to saving buildings, and upgrading them, rather than demolition and replacement. In response to pressures to preserve structures, particularly those with historical value, renovation promises to become big business, provided that current tax incentives are continued.

Past shifts from new construction to renovation and upgrading have often been short-term and responsive to temporary declines in the demand for new housing as credit tightened. The changes envisioned here are of longer duration and should be marked by the emergence of a new set of rehabilitation specialists who would constitute a less transient segment of the industry than in the past. In the financial markets, this development should stimulate the demand for residential improvement loans.

Conversion of rental to owned units such as condominiums, and additions and alterations to upgrade quality and add space, are but a few of the possibilites for adjusting the housing inventory to changing demographic trends and shifting preferences. ''Mingles housing,'' or the sharing of a single-family dwelling by two unrelated couples, offers another alternative. A couple that cannot afford a unit of its own may double up with another not only to share current expenses including mortgage payments but to split the down payment and other acquisition costs.

Yet another possibility is conversion to accommodate accessory apartments. The market for this type of living accommodation has grown remarkably. According to one estimate, more than a half million such units were ''constructed'' by remodeling and conversion between 1973 and 1980, an augmentation of the inventory that accounted for over 20% of all private unsubsidized rental construction during that period and more than double the proportion of the previous decade (Gellen, 1984, pp. 2, 76). In the early 1980s, that fraction rose to more than one-half (Gellen, 1984, p. 94).

Declining household size has given substantial impetus to the movement. Childless couples, primary in-

dividuals, unmarried adults, the middle-aged, and retired homeowners—all household types that have
increased in number and proportion during recent
years—are the sorts of people most likely to convert
space into accessory units.

Gellen estimates that somewhere between 10 million
and 18 million single-family units have surplus space
amenable to conversion. Converting only 15% of these
dwellings during the next 10 years would increase
production by over 150,000 units, enough to eliminate
the predicted shortfall in the construction of rental units
(Downs, 1983, pp. 121–126; Gellen, 1984, pp. 160–161).

Manufacturers and distributors of sophisticated
household equipment will play an increasingly important role among the suppliers of housing, regardless of
whether their products become legally parts of the real
estate. They will be the main developers of technological innovations and, while benefiting from expanding
demand, will also carry the risks always associated with
the innovative process. Tie-in arrangements between
equipment producers and home builders, so prominent
in the promotion of the all-electric kitchen, may become
more frequent.

Among other trends on the supply side, increasing
land costs are likely to lead to more compact housing developments with greater density per net acre in residential use. This projection assumes that the disproportionate price rise of residential sites will continue.[12] On the
criterion of open space, then, the quality of new housing units is apt to decline rather than improve. The real
luxury houses of the future will be mainly characterized
by conspicuous land consumption or, technically, a high
ratio of lot size to building coverage. But greater average density of residential developments does not affect

real investment which excludes the land component. Besides, the price increase for residential land may be somewhat moderated by two countervailing forces. One is the demographically induced decline in the number of newly built units, which should reduce the demands for sites. The other is the incipient migration of population from the large metropoles to smaller places. If this movement persists, some of the demand for land will shift from areas with typically high land prices to areas where land acquisition and site preparation are less costly.

Construction costs will also remain on an upward trend that constrains the extent of quality improvements, but they are likely to constitute a diminishing portion of total costs as the equipment component of the future dwelling gains in importance. The share of construction costs in total costs has already declined. In 1980, on-site labor and materials accounted for 50 cents per dollar of the total cost of new single-family houses as against 56 cents 10 years earlier (President's Commission on Housing, 1982, Table 13.1).

Residential building costs will in all probability not be reduced by major technological advances, however. After the disappointments of massive prefabrication, of the "Lustron" house so prominent during the veterans' emergency housing program of the postwar years, and of "Operation Breakthrough" sponsored by HUD in 1969–1975 to promote housing technology,[13] it is difficult to envision radical changes in the methods of residential construction. Ironically, productivity gains in the consumption of housing, the main trend projected in this chapter, are likely to outstrip productivity advances in the building of houses.

Charles Abrams, the late critic of our housing and cities, is credited with the wry comment that the residential construction industry survived the industrial revolution intact. This was, of course, an exaggeration. The building technology of today reflects numerous gradual improvements over that of a few decades ago (Eichler, 1982, pp. 62–78).[14] Such improvements will unquestionably continue.

The manufactured house has obtained a small but respectable position in the supply of new single-family dwellings and has had moderate success in overcoming consumer resistance; it will probably increase its market share in the future. There is even the possibility of a "reversed" technology transfer from Japan where house manufacture has made enormous progress (*Los Angeles Times*, 1984)—reversed because Japan's impressive industrialization is mostly based on technology initially transferred from this country and Europe.[15]

Nonetheless, one must be skeptical about the potential for intercountry technology transfers for an economic sector where it has so rarely happened, and probably for good reasons. The most notable exception has been the adoption of housing production techniques of advanced countries by the developing countries. This is not to deny the possibility that future transfers can be accomplished to the benefit of recipient economies. A case in point is self-help housing, and its close relative, sites and services programs, which harness the energies of the unemployed and the underemployed for building low-cost houses for the poor. After several decades of experience, the techniques for implementation are now well developed and have substantially eased the housing deficit in the Third World. While such self-help techniques have the greatest appeal in countries with large informal economies and reservoirs of unemployed, there are substantial opportunities for importing "software" technology

of this sort to solve the shelter problems of the burgeoning numbers of U.S. urban homeless, and self-help offers
an attractive alternative to the generally discredited solution of conventionally built public housing.

Turning to the future of *home building*, the likely
stabilization of the home ownership *rate* at the present
two-thirds of all occupied housing units does not mean
that home builders will be idle. The mere increase of
households will assure continuity, and replacement demand to make up losses from supply will reinforce the
demand from household formation to a moderate extent.
The increase of households in the 1985–1995 period is estimated at 13 million (Chapter 2). When the two-thirds
ratio is applied, the demand for new homes would be
8.7 million, or under 900,000 per year. This is below the
annual average of 1.1 million for single-family dwelling
starts during the 1970s, but still above the volume
reported in recent years of recession. Some portion of the
demand will be deflected from the single-family house
to condominiums and cooperatives in multifamily structures which offer the convenience of apartment living together with the tax and status benefits of ownership.
These types of units have already increased their share
in the ownership market and will continue to do so.[16]
Thus, the annual average of 900,000 new homes for
1985–1995 that was derived from the two-thirds ratio for
the housing stock may err on the high side. But it must
be stressed again that the real dollar volume of home
building is more relevant than the number of new units;
this volume will in all probability hold up better as quality improvements raise the amount of capital investment
per unit. Besides, the small home builders have the
opportunity of switching from new construction to al-

teration and modernization work which is projected to expand.

New investment in *rental housing* has become increasingly dependent on factors not related to expected profits from rental income alone. One of them is the see-saw tax legislation of the past two decades with respect to depreciation allowances, capital recovery periods, and tax rates on capital gains. Changes in these provisions had sometimes stimulating effects on rental housing investments (or investment generally) and opposite effects at other times. Recent policies and current official policy proposals have been in the same vein. Thus, the Economic Recovery Tax Act of 1981 significantly lowered the taxation of income-producing property by permitting accelerated depreciation on both new and existing buildings. Because of adverse effects on federal revenue, the Deficit Reduction Act of 1984 undid the 1981 legislation in part by lengthening the maximum depreciation period from 15 to 18 years. (For detail, see Kau and Sirmans, 1985.)

Various presidential and congressional bills under discussion at this writing provide for further, sizable extension of the depreciation period and other measures that would reduce the incentive to invest in income property. The current preferential treatment of residential real estate would be eliminated. (For detail, see Bank of America, 1985.)

Most of the time, previous alternations between liberal and restrictive taxation were not intended to, and did not in fact, improve the stability of rental investment but resulted from shifting general fiscal policies. On the contrary, they had destabilizing effects when investors expected legislative changes. Recently, for example, rental housing construction has been greatly stimulated by the anticipated tightening of tax provisions, reinforcing the inevitable slump when the tightening actually occurs. In the long run, a favorable climate for rental housing requires reasonably constant taxation.

Rental housing has also become a popular investment by high-income taxpayers seeking tax shelter rather than competitive returns from rental income. There is growing sentiment for closing the loopholes that promote tax shelter—again because of the need for raising federal revenues.[17] Further, many rental projects have been built in anticipation of capital gains from later conversion to condominiums, so low rental income during the interim period did not act as a deterrent.

Apart from the uncertainties of future tax rules, investment has also been impeded by the specter of rent control. For the first time in American history, many localities in recent years have adopted rent regulation in the absence of a war emergency and general price controls. While newly built units are always exempt from control, investors are apprehensive over the possibility that their projects may be subjected to it in the future.

At the same time, the demand for rental housing is likely to increase as the rate of home ownership stabilizes. According to one authoritative estimate, the demand for new rental units in the 1980s will come to 600,000 per year (Downs, 1983, p. 7 and pp. 62–72). This number exceeds by far the volume produced in any 10-year period on record, although it was sometimes attained in a single year such as 1983. Still, the same forecast predicts annual production of only 475,000 units (Downs, 1983, pp. 121–126). The shortfall can be expected to push rents upward and, indeed, that may be the soundest and most durable remedy for restoring the profitability of rental housing from rental income alone, without the crutches of tax shelter or special income tax benefits.[18]

Balancing the plus factors supporting a fairly strong rental market are the minuses. Most are demographic. Young and old householders have the highest propensity to rent. The burgeoning middle-aged groups, and particularly the senior middle-aged segment—consisting of the baby boomers who have advanced into middle age and beyond—already own their homes and are unlikely to become tenants soon. And there is the expressed desire of a vast majority of Americans for ownership as a high-ranking personal goal. According to the Joint Center survey cited earlier, "81 percent of current owners who plan to move in the next five years and 70 percent of current renters believe that their next dwelling unit will be a single-family, detached house" (MIT–Harvard Joint Center for Urban Studies, 1984, p. 2).

Added to this is the increasing importance of immigration as a growth factor and the changing composition of population flowing from abroad. Immigration, in both its legal and illegal components, now accounts for roughly one-half of total population gains. As the numbers have grown, the origin of immigrants has shifted. During the 1950s, over half were Europeans; today only one in five of the new arrivals are. The drop has been more than offset by the skyrocketing numbers of Asians, whose share of the total rose more than five-fold. Although the immigrants' first accommodations in the new land once were likely to be rented, many soon became owners. The notoriously high propensity for property ownership among Asians should further bolster the demand for single-family dwellings.

To cushion adverse effects of market rents on lower-income people, a housing allowance program along the lines of the HUD experiment deserves high priority as soon as the federal government's fiscal position improves.[19] Since most of the states are in reasonably good financial condition, they may introduce housing allowance programs of their own, or the cost may be shared between the federal and state governments. In any event, a policy shift from supporting rental housing as such through tax loopholes to better-targeted programs in favor of lower-income tenants would be highly desirable. Meanwhile, the emergence of a serious rental-housing crisis—often prematurely or without real cause invoked in past years—is a distinct possibility.

The *second home* for vacation and weekend use was once seen as an immensely promising growth market. One can say from general observation that it has been an expanding market. An increasing number of well-to-do households are maintaining a condominium in Aspen, Colorado, or a unit in Sea Island, South Carolina, or both, in addition to their main residence. The time-shared condominium ownership in resort places has broadened the appeal of the second home. Unfortunately, no data are available on the extent to which the hopes for a growth market have materialized. Second homes are statistically buried in the number of units classified by the Bureau of the Census as seasonally vacant. Besides, many second homes have been created through conversion of existing rural structures rather than new construction, a process that at best raises residential investment by capital spending on rehabilitation if it is reported. With economic progress, the second home will probably become more popular in the future, but its contribution to market activity will be constrained if official tax proposals limiting the deduction of mortgage interest payments are adopted.

Mobile homes are unlikely to play a significant role in the future of housing. The record of mobile home production in the United States is not encouraging. Annual shipments to dealers in recent years have declined sharply from the peak level of 1972–1973, when they reached an annual volume of nearly 600,000, to an average of 266,000 a year in 1976–1979, a boom period for regular home building, and under 240,000 in the early 1980s. One might have expected that the house price inflation of the late 1970s would turn frustrated home buyers to the competitively priced mobile home, or that the severe business downturn of 1980–1982 would have a similar effect. Neither happened.

The poor performance of mobile homes as substitutes for conventional units reflects, of course, the fact that the great differential in acquisition costs is not matched in periodic financial charges. Although FHA and VA now insure mortgages on these homes and some lenders provide conventional financing, most credit is still obtained by consumer loans with shorter maturities and carrying higher interest rates. The evidence suggests also that the mobile home caters to a relatively specialized clientele.[20]

According to the Annual Housing Surveys, mobile homes have accounted for nearly 5% of all occupied housing units since 1973. This market share is unlikely to increase much in the remainder of this century. Some modest stimulus may come from recent improvements in the market environment for "candominiums" or "tin cans on wheels," as they are less charitably dubbed. Many communities have relaxed the zoning restrictions that formerly confined mobile homes to remote areas sometimes called "galvanized ghettos." Designs have been upgraded with stucco and wood-clad exteriors and with windows decorated by shutters to make the units resemble conventional dwellings and broaden their acceptability. At a recent home show, a two-story, four-bedroom Victorian-style house complete with garage and cupola was displayed as one example of these possibilities (Rivera, 1984, p. 1). And it was available for under $110,000, towed to the site and assembled.

In addition, "manufactured houses" not on wheels are offered by large builders who see opportunities for scale economies from off-site production using assembly-line methods in closed factories that operate in any kind of weather. Cheaper labor than that employed in conventional construction drives costs down. Other large-scale builders have sought economies by fabricating components on the site.

THE GENERAL ECONOMIC CLIMATE

The projected emphasis on quality improvements in both new housing and the stock of existing housing raises the question whether general economic conditions through the rest of this century will support such a trend. Hence, the outlook for economic growth in the next decade and a half becomes a crucial issue. Comprehensive statistical estimates for so long a period must be viewed with a great deal of skepticism even if they are based on econometric models. The results depend on assumptions concerning critical traditional variables determining economic growth, such as productivity advances, the propensity for business investment in plant and equipment, the competitiveness of U.S. products in world markets, and the prospect for jobs and gains in real consumer income. At this juncture, however, other factors more amenable to analysis have also an important bearing on the long-run performance of the American economy. Prominent among these are two phenomena that are currently in the forefront of public and professional discussion and have given rise to considerable apprehension over this nation's economic future: the unprecedented federal budget deficit and the enormous indebtedness of non-OPEC developing countries to commercial banks in the United States.

These structural maladjustments are especially germane to the future economic climate. During much of the period to the year 2000, the federal deficit and the threat of an international financial crisis will greatly affect the potentials for economic growth and for the material progress of American consumers. The twin problems of the federal deficit and overextended intercountry borrowings have a direct influence on the future level of interest rates which are of such strategic importance to the housing sector. Are they in danger of stifling the growth of our economy to the point that the projection of a strong trend toward improved housing quality becomes a pipe dream? The question is all the more serious since the problems are universally recognized as lending themselves to no short-term solutions and requiring forceful (as well as painful) action by policy-makers to blunt their impact on this country's economic welfare.

Turning first to the federal deficit, the Deficit Reduction Act of 1984 signified at least the recognition that measures to cut its size are an urgent part of the national agenda. True, the three-year package of tax increases estimated at $50 billion and spending cuts estimated at $11 billion is barely sufficient to keep the deficit from rising, but this was no small achievement on the eve of national elections, usually a most inopportune moment for legislating higher taxes and lower federal expenditures. A fiscal policy that would produce significant inroads into the deficit is still to be developed, however. From the viewpoint of housing and other investment, the important point is that every billion of deficit reduction makes the federal government a supplier of funds to the money and capital markets to the tune of a billion, reversing its position of the past few years as a net demander of funds. Other things equal, such a reversal should have beneficial effects on interest rates as well as the availability of investment capital for the private sector. But the mix of tax increases and spending cuts in measures to lower the deficit will have some considerable impact on the demand for higher-quality housing. The smaller the share of higher taxes borne directly or indirectly by consumers, the better the prospect that the potential for housing quality improvements will materialize.

Bolder steps to reduce the deficit will also enable the Federal Reserve System to pursue a more accommodating monetary policy in the long run, apart from the ups and downs of the business cycle. The recent evolution of the housing finance system itself, by broadening the ultimate sources of mortgage money, should promote a steadier supply of funds.[21] Hence, it appears that future housing market activity is not so much jeopardized by scarcity of loanable funds as it is by prohibitive interest rates. To the extent that deficit reduction converts the federal government to a net supplier of funds to the capital market, interest rates should become more favorable for borrowers seeking loans for residential construction and the renovation of existing dwellings. Under these circumstances, the need for alternative mortgage instruments offering low initial financing charges but involving higher later costs and risks to both borrowers and lenders would be lessened.[22] The beneficial short-term effects of declining interest rates on housing demand have once more been demonstrated in 1985–1986, even in the presence of an undiminished federal deficit. For the long run, however, the deficit remains an impediment to low mortgage interest rates and therefore to a healthy climate for housing markets.

The international debt problem—the first major issue of this kind since World War II—affects the nation's economic growth in many ways that are sketched here only to make a single point: Its link to the future of American housing is not as tenuous as may appear. Growth could be retarded through de facto default on the enormous debt owned to private U.S. banks, a calamity so far avoided only by an admixture of new loans, some accounting legerdemain, and substantial assistance by the International Monetary Fund. Yet rescheduling and rolling over the debt only defers payments of interest and principal to the day when the borrowing countries have an international-account surplus large enough to meet them—a time that seems remote for the principal outstanding.

Meanwhile, interest payments are the critical problem. Since they constitute a sizable portion of the creditor banks' total income and net worth, default could impair the capacity of our banking system to meet domestic loan demands or, more likely, the demands would be met by rationing funds at higher interest rates than would prevail otherwise. If the Federal Reserve were to provide enough reserves to the affected banks to prevent such a contingency, the money supply would increase beyond the range set to satisfy normal needs, with the result that the specter of inflation might reappear.

Ironically, economic growth in this country could also be retarded if the debtor countries performed the miracle of meeting their interest payments on schedule. The main if not the only means by which the debtor nations can transfer large amounts of interest (let alone principal) to the United States is a massive expansion of their exports to earn the hard currency needed. This solution would not only incur the risk of throttling the domestic development of the debtor countries to the point of threatening social unrest and political instability but would have adverse effects on our own economy by flooding American markets with imports of manufactured goods.[23] In response, domestic pressures for protectionist measures, already strong, would intensify. Should they be successful, consumers would be shortchanged and the efficiencies obtained from untrammeled international trade would be reduced. If not, domestic jobs would be lost in our smokestack industries, textile production, and even the assembly of electronic components, aggravating the experience of the past few years. The only remedy would be a strong improvement of U.S. exports, discussed below.

In any event, the consequences of the international debt problem heighten uncertainty about the future, and uncertainty is a great enemy of economic growth and stability, abhorred by the financial community, and an impediment to the confidence required for material progress. For this if no other reason, the present patchwork of ad hoc measures to avert a crisis may need to be replaced by a concerted program of guarantees if not loan assistance involving the U.S. government directly or through international financial agencies, or both. If so, any U.S. outlays commensurate with the magnitude of the problem would retard the reduction of the federal deficit and raise the level of interest rates. Nevertheless, a concerted program seems to be the lesser of two evils since it would moderate if not remove the uncertainty now hanging over the international debt issue like the proverbial sword of Damocles. In conclusion, this issue need not endanger U.S. economic growth conducive to improved housing if early action is taken to deal with it constructively, regardless of disputes over who is to blame for its genesis in the first place.

Compared to the federal deficit and the potential threat posed by an international debt crisis, other current maladjustments seem more amenable to solutions. The U.S. trade deficit that has dragged down domestic employment is partly if not largely the result of a sharp rise in the exchange rate of the dollar relative to other key currencies since 1980. This increase is in the process of correction. From February 1985 to March 1986, the tradeweighted value of the dollar dropped by about 30%.

The mere demonstration that it *can* decline is apt to exert further downward pressure as foreign holders, especially the "safe-haven" holders, realize that their dollar balances cannot be expected to appreciate indefinitely and adjust their currency transactions accordingly.[24] Thus, at least one of the causes of the trade deficit is losing its potency. A sustained reduction in the dollar's exchange value would strengthen U.S. exports and weaken the profitability of importing goods to this country. It would also help correct the recent change of the United States from a net creditor to a net debtor in international accounts by enhancing the nation's ability to export its products competitively to world markets.

Still another maladjustment is the recent turmoil in domestic financial markets, in the wake of widely publicized losses and reorganizations of the banking and savings and loan systems, combined with a deregulation policy excessive in scope or speed, or both. If the resulting uncertainties should be allowed to continue for long, the housing market might suffer from financial constraints. This effect has so far been avoided. The timely rescue operations of the federal deposit insurance agencies have served to prevent any serious impairment of public confidence in our financial structure.

As for deregulation, legislative and regulatory efforts are under way to replace the patchwork of ad hoc, poorly coordinated measures with a firm new framework determining the activities that the various types of financial institutions and subsidiaries of nonfinancial firms are authorized to conduct. If these efforts succeed in the near future and if the recent interest rate declines are not reversed for any prolonged period, housing should be spared the consequences of financial disorder.

On the positive side, the ongoing deregulation has already broadened the sources of loanable funds by drawing nontraditional mortgage investors into the market, mainly through the progressive conversion of mortgage packages into marketable securities more suited to the investment practices of pension and other funds which are averse to small individual mortgage transactions. The new sources have more than offset the weakened participation of savings institutions which once dominated housing finance. This shift can be expected to continue regardless of what form the final deregulation of the financial system may take.

As a final note on the future scenario, we return to a demographic force, the main thrust of this study. According to Easterlin's analysis of generational changes (Chapter 3), the economic fortune of the generation that is now beginning to enter the labor force and the housing market should be better off than that of the preceding one because it is smaller. As the labor supply is reduced, prospects for employment and advancement should be brighter and wage and salary levels should be higher. This hypothesis rests, of course, on the expectation that the demand for labor and the opportunities for self-employment continue to expand, i.e., that labor supply will become more scarce relative to demand. If the potential impediments of the federal deficit and the international debt problem are overcome, there seems to be no reason why this part of the scenario would fail to materialize. True, robotization of some manufacturing processes will displace manual workers, and some of the classic American industries no longer provide the plentiful jobs of yesteryear. But manufacture now accounts for only 20% of total employment, far less than the service sector. While service wages are generally lower than wages in manufacture, fast-growing professional service occupations pay at least as well as skilled industrial jobs. If history is any guide, technological and structural changes in the American economy have always been accompanied by aggregate economic growth despite transitional problems affecting specific groups of people and business firms.

Barring catastrophic events, there is every reason to believe that history will repeat itself. The housing sector will mirror the general experience. The prospective decline of household growth will in all probability reduce the number of jobs in new residential construction, but the projected trend toward quality improvements will create other job opportunities in the production and distribution of household equipment and in the upgrading of large parts of the existing housing stock.

APPENDIX F: DETAILED DATA ON CONSUMER PURCHASING POWER AND ON HOMEOWNERSHIP

TABLE F.1. Contributions to Changes in Total Consumer Purchasing Power (ΔPP) by Changes in Number of Households (ΔHH) and per Household Incomes (ΔY), by 5-Year Intervals, 1970–1995 (Amounts in Millions of 1980 Dollars)

| | | $ Contribution to ΔPP | | % Contribution to ΔPP | |
Interval	ΔPP	ΔHH	ΔY	ΔHH	ΔY
1970–1975	$155,695	$163,747	– $8,052	105.2%	– 5.2%
1975–1980	200,130	202,479	– 2,348	101.2	– 1.2
1980–1985	248,295	175,355	72,941	70.6	29.4
1985–1990	381,026	173,596	207,430	45.6	54.4
1990–1995	416,737	663,747	252,989	39.3	60.7

[a]Sources: 1970–1980, U.S. Bureau of the Census (1984a) Table 3; 1985–1995 projections based on estimates in Data Resources, Inc. (1983). Income data reported in 1982$ and converted to 1980$. Income projections based on rates of growth projected by DRI from 1980 census figures; household projections are averages of the census B and D series.

TABLE F.2. Homeownership Rate by Age of Household Head and Median Household Income of Homeowners, 1983[a,b]

Type of household and age of head	Median income of household	Ownership rate
Married couples		
Under 25	$19,900	31.0%
25–29	27,100	53.0
30–34	30,300	70.2
35–44	33,700	81.1
45–64	32,300	87.3
65 and over	16,100	86.1
Other families, male head		
Under 45	25,700	35.4
45–64	27,400	69.8
65 and over	15,600	76.6
Other families, female head		
Under 45	16,100	29.1
45–64	17,500	62.2
65 and over	13,400	71.8
One-person households, male head		
Under 45	22,700	29.5
45–64	19,300	45.4
65 and over	9,300	59.1
One-person households, female head		
Under 45	18,300	20.6
45–64	11,100	58.3
65 and over	7,100	61.0

[a]Earlier reports of the source do not show an adequate age classification of households other than married couples. The relationship between age of household head, median income, and the homeownership rate seems to be quite stable over time.
[b]Source: U.S. Bureau of the Census, *Annual Housing Survey*, 1984b, Part C, table A-1.

NOTES

1. The household income estimates are those of Data Resources, Inc., after adjustment by the authors.
2. The literature is large and growing; see for example Ellickson *et al.* (1977), Follain and Malpezzi (1980), Kain and Quigley (1970), Merrill (1980), Noland (1980), Rosen (1974), Smith and Ohsfeldt (1979), and Wilkinson (1976).
3. Prices of new technology characteristically drop fast and efficiency rises quickly. It has been calculated that "if the aircraft industry had evolved as spectacularly as the computer industry over the past 25 years, a Boeing 747 would cost $50 today, and it would circle the globe in 20 minutes on 5 gallons of fuel. Such performance would represent a rough analogue of the reduction of cost, the increase in speed of operation and the decrease in energy consumption of computers" (Toong and Gupta, 1982). Some new devices may not find a market, however. The classic example is the Video-phone developed by RCA in 1964 that offered people communicating over the phone the opportunity to be seen as well as heard. Consumers (as well as business firms) decided that the price for the privilege of seeing their counterparts was too high or they did not care for the privilege.
4. In addition to the well-known statistics demonstrating progress in the equipment of the average house, recent Surveys of Consumer Finances hint that average home *values*, as distinct from *prices*, are rising—at least at the upper end of the distribution. A review of the 1983 survey, the most recent, evaluates the data on changing values as follows: "While nominal housing prices continued to rise between 1977 and 1983 (after more than doubling between 1970 and 1977), the *median* value of homes declined 5 percent in real terms over this six-year interval. Interestingly, in face of this decline, the *mean* real home value increased" (Avery *et al.*, 1984, p. 684, emphasis added). An increase in the proportion of more expensive homes likely explains the difference in mean and median changes. For example, during the 6-year period the proportion of families owning homes valued at $150,000 or more, in constant (1983) dollars, doubled from 4 to 8%.
5. In 1980, for example, 32.8 million owner-occupied units showed occupancy of only 0.5 persons or less per room. The corresponding figure for renter-occupied units was 15.6 million. Units with such low occupancy accounted for 62.5% of all owned units and 56.5% of all rented units (U.S. Bureau of the Census, 1981, Part A).
6. The Annual Housing Surveys are based on a limited sample and are therefore subject to larger margins of error than the data from the decennial

census. A third source, the quarterly vacancy surveys of the Bureau of the Census, show even a recent decline of the homeownership rate, from 64.5% in I-1984 to 64.1% in I-1985. Because of the procedures needed for obtaining these estimates and the small decrease, the results should be viewed with caution. See U.S. Bureau of the Census (1985b).

7. Figures from U.S. Bureau of the Census, *Annual Housing Surveys* (various years), Part D.

8. The refusal of many landlords to accept or retain married couples with small children has contributed to this trend, but it was probably not a major factor.

9. Renters were not only poorer but they were likely to get poorer housing for their rental dollar. According to Downs (1984, p. IV-5), "The vast majority of Americans are well-housed. Only 7.5 percent of all metropolitan area households occupied inadequate dwellings in 1983. But 17.2 percent of poor metropolitan area *renter* households lived in such units; another 6.4 percent were overcrowded. These last two groups comprised a total of 1.3 million households."

10. The homeownership rate of single-spouse families fell from 48.2% in 1973 to 45.1% in 1983. The rate for single-person households was 44.5 in 1973, 42.3 in 1977, and 46.5 in 1983. The rate for married couples showed a nearly continuous increase from 74 to 77% between 1973 and 1983.

11. For a theoretical analysis that considers new construction and modifications of the existing stock of dwellings as substitute forms of supply response, see Rothenberg (1985).

12. Between 1970 and 1980, the land component in the cost of new single-family dwellings increased by 248% compared to 176% for total cost including financing and builders' profit (President's Commission on Housing, 1982, Table 13.1). According to FHA data, the average lot value of new single-family homes rose from $1.24 per square foot in 1976 to nearly $2.00 in 1980–1983, despite the severe housing recession of 1980–1982. The complex reasons for the increased land costs are summarized in President's Commission on Housing (1982), pp. 180–182.

13. For an evaluation of Operation Breakthrough, see U.S. General Accounting Office, 1976.

14. Yet, for the entire construction industry, productivity declined between 1968 and 1978 by 2.8% annually, compared to an average growth of 2.4% per annum during the previous 18 years. Slow growth in capital per worker appears to be the culprit (Stokes, 1981).

15. Using highly sophisticated and technologically advanced methods, Japanese builders produce panels and modules with the aid of computerized and robotized systems. The components are delivered to the site at substantial cost savings to the buyer. The great bulk of sales, it is claimed,

are made to first-time buyers who in Japan average 42 years of age. But whether the technology can be transferred to this country is an open question.

16. Between 1975 and 1983, the number of owner-occupied units in condominiums and cooperatives increased from 869,000 to 1.7 million, or from 1.8% of all year-round owner-occupied units to 3.2% (U.S. Bureau of the Census, *Annual Housing Survey*, various). The figures include units regardless of type of structure and those converted from rental status as well as new construction.

17. For example, the president's tax program of 1985 would limit interest deductions by investors in real estate partnerships or syndicates to the amount "at risk," i.e., the amount actually invested. Currently, these deductions apply to borrowings by the partnership as well as the partners' own investment—one of the main ingredients of "tax shelter."

18. For more detailed analyses of rental housing, see Downs (1983) and Lowry (1982).

19. For extensive analyses of the experiment, see Friedman and Weinberg, (1983), Lowry (1983), and Struyk and Bendix (1981).

20. About 60% of all year-round mobile homes were located outside metropolitan areas in 1980–1983. The median household income of occupants has been considerably lower than that of all households in both the homeownership and rental categories.

21. For detail, see Federal Home Loan Mortgage Corporation (1984).

22. For a critical appraisal of alternative mortgage instruments, see Kendall (1984).

23. Because of multilateral international merchandise transactions, U.S. import increases would not necessarily equal the exports by the debtor countries. Nevertheless, a large portion of the latter's exports would be directed to the United States, which accounts for such a large part of world markets.

24. According to Klugman's recent (1985) working paper for the National Bureau of Economic Research, the strong dollar is unsustainable because part of its strength must be viewed as a speculative bubble which is bound to burst.

REFERENCES

Avery, R. B., Elliehausen, G. E., and Canner, G. B. (1984). Survey of consumer finances, 1984. *Federal Reserve Bulletin, 70*(9), 679–692.

Baer, W. C. (1979). Empty housing space—An overlooked resource. *Policy Studies Journal, 8*(2), 220–227.

Bank of America. (1985, August). *The president's tax proposal and real estate.* Residential Mortgage Banking Economic Report, San Francisco.

Barnett, C. L. (1979). *Using hedonic indexes to measure housing quantity.* Santa Monica, CA: Rand Corporation.

Data Resources, Inc. (1983). *Demographic-economic model: Forecast summary.* Lexington, MA: Author.

Downs, A. (1983). *Rental housing in the 1980s.* Washington, D.C.: Brookings Institution.

Downs, A. (1984). Blueprint for a fairer housing policy: Subsidize low-income renters, not first-time home buyers. *Los Angeles Times,* September 16.

Eichler, N. (1982). *The merchant builders.* Cambridge, MA: M.I.T. Press.

Ellickson, B. B., Fisherman, B., and Morrison, P. (1977). *Economic analysis of urban housing markets.* Santa Monica, CA: Rand Corporation.

Federal Home Loan Mortgage Corporation. (1984). *Secondary mortgage markets* (February and May).

Follain, J. R., and Malpezzi, S. (1980). *Dissecting housing value and rent: Estimates of hedonic indexes for thirty-nine large SMSAs.* Washington, D.C.: Urban Institute.

Friedman, J., and Weinberg, D. (1983). *The great housing experiment.* Beverly Hills, CA: Sage.

Gellen, M. (1983). *Underutilization in American housing: Residential space standards and social change.* Working Paper 339. Berkeley, CA: Institute of Urban and Regional Development, University of California.

Gellen, M. (1984). *More than one: Accessory apartments in single-family housing.* Berkeley, CA: Department of City and Regional Planning, University of California. (Processed)

Glick, P. (1977). Updating the life cycle of the family. *Journal of Marriage and the Family, 39*(1), 5–13.

Kain, J. F., and Quigley, J. M. (1970). Measuring the value of housing quality. *Journal of the American Statistical Association, 64,* 532–548.

Kau, J. B., and Sirmans, C. F. (1985). *Tax planning for real estate investors* (3rd ed.). Englewood Cliffs, NJ: Prentice-Hall.

Kendall, L. T. (1984). Caution: Innovation at work. *Secondary mortgage markets* (May).

Klugman, P. R. (1985). *Is the strong dollar sustainable?* Working Paper No. 1644. Cambridge, MA: National Bureau of Economic Research.

Linder, S. B. (1970). *The harried leisure class.* New York: Columbia University Press.

Los Angeles Times. (1984). Japanese Americans meet to talk housing. Financial Section, February 16.

Lowry, I. S. (1982). *Rental housing in the 1970s: Searching for the crisis.* Santa Monica, CA: Rand Corporation.

Lowry, I. S. (Ed.). (1983). *Experimenting with housing allowances: Findings of a ten-year study of housing assistance for low-income families, with implications for national housing policy.* Cambridge, MA: Oelgeschlager, Gunn & Gain.

Markusen, A. (1983). The lonely squandering of urban time. In J. Zimmerman (Ed.), *The technological woman: Interfacing with tomorrow.* New York: Prager Press.

Merrill, S. R. (1980). *Hedonic indices as a measure of housing quality.* Cambridge, MA: Abt Associates.

MIT–Harvard Joint Center for Urban Studies. (1984). *Joint Center Report,* No. 34 (June).

Nilles, J. (1976). *The telecommunications-transportation tradeoff: Options for tomorrow.* New York: Wiley.

Noland, C. W. (1980). *Hedonic indexes for St. Joseph County, Indiana.* Santa Monica, CA: Rand Corporation.

Pennisi, E. (1985). Her house is her computer castle. *Los Angeles Times,* September 22.

President's Commission on Housing. (1982). *The report of the President's Commission on Housing.* Washington, D.C.: Author.

Rempel, W. C. (1985). Electronic mail: A revolutionary carrier aims to become routine. *Los Angeles Times,* February 24.

Rivera, N. (1984). Homes from factories—A new image. *Los Angeles Times,* January 6.

Robinson, J. (1980). Housework technology and household work. In S. F. Berk (Ed.), *Women and household labor.* Beverly Hills, CA: Sage.

Rosen, S. (1974). Hedonic prices and implicit markets: Product differentiation in pure competition. *Journal of Political Economy, 82,* 34–55.

Rothenberg, J. (1985). New construction vs. rehabilitation: The tradeoff in meeting America's housing needs. Working Paper No. 85–92. Berkeley, CA: Center for Real Estate and Urban Economics.

Scott, J. W. (1982). Mechanization of women's work. *Scientific American, 247*(September), 167–187.

Smith, B. A., and Ohsfeldt, R. (1979). Housing price inflation in Houston: 1970 to 1976. *Policy Studies Journal, 8*(2), 257–276.

Stokes, H. K., Jr. (1981). An examination of the productivity decline in the construction industry. *Review of Economics and Statistics, 63*(4), 495–502.

Struyk, R. J., and Bendix, M. (Eds.). (1981). *Housing vouchers for the poor: Lessons from a national experiment.* Washington, D.C.: Urban Institute.

Szalai, A. (1966). Multinational comparative social research. *American Behavioral Scientist, 18*(4).

Toffler, A. (1980). *The third wave.* New York: Bantam.

Toong, H.-M. D. and Gupta, A. (1982). Personal computers. *Scientific American, 247*(3), 86–107.

U.S. Bureau of the Census. (1975). *Historical statistics of the United States: Colonial times to 1970.* Washington, D.C.: U.S. Government Printing Office.

U.S. Bureau of the Census. (1981). *Annual housing survey: 1980.* Washington, D.C.: U.S. Government Printing Office.

U.S. Bureau of the Census. (1984a). *Money income of households, families, and persons in the United States: 1982.* Current Population Reports, Series P-60, No. 142. Washington, D.C.: U.S. Government Printing Office.

U.S. Bureau of the Census. (1984b). *Annual housing survey.* Washington, D.C.: U.S. Government Printing Office.

U.S. Bureau of the Census. (1985a). *Statistical abstract of the United States: 1985.* Washington, D.C.: U.S. Government Printing Office.

U.S. Bureau of the Census. (1985b). *Housing vacancies, first quarter 1985,* Series H-111. Washington, D.C.: U.S. Government Printing Office.

U.S. Department of Commerce. (various). *Value of new construction put in place.* Washington, D.C.: U.S. Government Printing Office.

U.S. Department of Housing and Urban Development. (1980). *The conversion of rental housing to condominiums and cooperatives: A national study of scope, causes and impacts.* Washington, D.C.: U.S. Government Printing Office.

U.S. General Accounting Office. (1976). *Operation breakthrough—Lessons learned about demonstrating new technology.* Report to the Congress. Washington, D.C.: U.S. Government Printing Office.

Vanek, J. (1978). Household technology and social status and residence differences in housework. *Technology and Culture, 19.*

Wilkinson, R. K., with Archer, C. A. (1976). The quality of housing and the measurement of long-term changes in housing prices. *Urban Studies, 13.*

Index

193